the handmade soap book

melinda coss

photography by emma peios

For my soaplist buddies:
May all their bubbles be bountiful.

New Holland Publishers (UK) Ltd
London • Cape Town • Sydney • Auckland
www.newhollandpublishers.com

Garfield House, 86-88 Edgware Road
London W2 2 EA
United Kingdom

80 McKenzie Street
Cape Town 8001
South Africa

Unit 1, 66 Gibbes Street
Chatswood, NSW 2067
Australia

218 Lake Road
Northcote, Auckland
New Zealand

ISBN 978 1 85974 006 4

14 16 18 17 15 13

Editor: Jane Struthers
Design and Art Direction: Blackjacks
Photographer: Emma Peios
Managing Editor: Coral Walker

Reproduction by Modern Age Repro House Ltd, Hong Kong
Printed and bound in Singapore by Tien Wah Press (Pte) Ltd

acknowledgements
The author would like to thank the following people for their valuable contributions to this book: Yvonne McFarlane for faith and hope (no
charity required), Coral Walker for stylish overseeing of the whole shebang, Jane Struthers for creative nitpicking, Emma Peios for her stunning
photos, Jack Buchan for a great book design, Elaine White for her saponification table, Elaya Tsosie for her hair care information, House of
Crafts for supplying moulds and glycerine soap, Verdant for colouring liquid, moulds and glycerine soap, Lush for their Floating Bath Soak
recipe and all my friends and neighbours for guinea pig services.

To give you the option of working in either ounces or grams, it has been necessary to round up or down the
conversion figure slightly. These small differences will not affect your end result.
Use either ounces or grams, but do not mix the two in a recipe.

contents

introd

'You're turning into a witch!' proclaimed my neighbour, Judy, when she found me, on a moonlit evening, stirring a cauldron full of deliciously fragrant soap. To the uninitiated it is difficult to explain the pleasures of watching a pot full of oils change into a rich, creamy substance, but I am not alone in experiencing this: soapmakers, the world over, will tell you that this hobby is outrageously addictive.

While all the recipes in this book (unless stated otherwise) are my very own concoctions, my list-mates who I have met on the Internet have provided an endless source of inspiration. The daily exchanges of information have been so friendly and useful that this book should be considered a group effort.

Once you see the ingredients used in these recipes I will not have to persuade you of the goodness of handmade soaps, nor the reasons for making them. What could be better than creating a soap that will work wonderfully with your personal skin type and provide you with your favourite fragrance and texture at the same time?

This book will explain the processes and give you food for thought and experimentation. I have offered the recipes in 2-lb (900 g) batches but you can halve or double these as required. Do not, however, alter the ingredients without reading the section on oils (see pages 14-16) and please take the time to read 'The ten commandments' on page 13 before attempting to make your first batch.

I hope you will enjoy making and using the soap recipes in this book and that you will be inspired to create some exciting concoctions of your own. Soapmaking is one of the few ways you can really make a mess, enjoy yourself and stay clean, all at the same time. Happy soaping.

Melinda Coss

uction

the history of soapmaking

Marketing directors worldwide will tell you that, in order to sell a new product, people must be convinced that:

❏ It will enhance their sex drive.
❏ It will lengthen their lives.
❏ They will be socially unacceptable without it.

And so it came to pass that some biblical whizzkid spotted a gap in the market and proclaimed 'Cleanliness is next to godliness', sending people the world over in search of purifying and cleansing agents (see Jeremiah 2:22 and Malachi 3:2) with which to improve their lot.

In those early days, tree bark and herbs such as soapwort were used to enhance ablutions, but in the 8th century, the Italians and the Spanish set about creating what we now call soap from goat fat and beech tree ash. The French (a stylish bunch of people) introduced the concept of replacing the animal fat – or tallow – with olive oil, while the pioneers of America traditionally treated soapmaking as a homecraft, creating sodium hydroxide (caustic soda/lye) by leaving rainwater to drip through a perforated barrel filled with hardwood ash. The resulting solution was then boiled until it was concentrated enough for a fresh egg (still in its shell) to float on the surface without sinking. Fat was rendered from whichever animals happened to be around at the time and grandma-style soap was created, although rough skin and holey socks were often unwelcome by-products of this rather caustic brew.

In England, in the early 17th century, the soap industry was developing at a rapid pace and King James I (a man very supportive of small businesses) granted soapmakers special privileges. By 1791, the French were ahead again with the discovery, by the chemist Nicolas Leblanc, of a process that extracted soda from ordinary salt. By this time the findings of Louis Pasteur had also firmly established that personal cleanliness reduced the spread of disease and the 'hygienic movement' was born.

Andrew Pears was one of the first people to define the need for soap as a cosmetic aid. The son of a Cornish farmer, he trained as a hairdresser and then established himself in his own salon in London's Soho where he also manufactured and sold rouges and other cosmetics. He set about refining the existing harsh base soaps and eventually produced a transparent soap perfumed with 'the flowers of an English garden'. In 1835 Andrew brought his grandson, Francis Pears, into the business. Francis became his partner, a relationship which continued until 1838 when Andrew retired.

Some years later, Francis's son-in-law, Thomas J Barratt, joined the company as a partner and brought with him the flair and marketing skills required to turn Pears' Soap into a worldwide commodity.

At this time, advertising was a revolutionary new concept and Barratt's creative schemes met much opposition. Undeterred, he mounted huge campaigns to inform the public that Pears' Soap was safe, healthy and, above all, made its users beautiful. His marketing projects were bold and costly but undoubtedly contributed enormously to the success of the company.

Barratt's use of John Everett Millais' painting *Bubbles* as an advertising poster promoting the soaps was only one of a number of enterprising schemes that, even today, trigger an immediate association with Pears' Soap.

For those born in the reign of the seldom amused and extremely modest Queen Victoria, the concept of a naked body-bath was decadent in the extreme (it was only in the second half of the 20th century that the idea of a daily bath was no longer considered both harmful and sinful). However, it was during Victoria's reign that the entrepreneur WH Lever began the mass-production and marketing of soap. He established, as his base, a large factory and a new town, situated close to the River Mersey in northern England, which he named Port Sunlight. It was built specifically for the housing and welfare of his employees.

The late 20th century has spawned a revival for things natural and a renewed interest in herbal remedies. Many people seek to preserve the environment and to reduce the use of toxins and chemicals. The establishment and success of such organizations as The Body Shop have raised public awareness of the virtues of using natural cosmetics. The strong principles of its founder, Anita Roddick, have also demonstrated that it is possible for women to build empires from small enterprises.

An exciting soap venture resulting from The Body Shop is proving very successful for Mark Constantine, another British entrepreneur, who has opened a fast-growing chain of retail soap 'delis' under the name of Lush. Mark began in 1974, creating herbal hair and beauty treatments. He went on to form a creative partnership with Anita Roddick, originating and developing products for The Body Shop. He was their main supplier for over 15 years but, in 1994, launched his first shop in Poole marketing soaps and bath products made mainly from fresh fruit and vegetables, essential oils and 'safe' synthetics. Mark is co-owner of the enterprise and considers his success to be the result of good team-work. The Lush products have wonderfully zany names like Angels on Bareskin and Dream Cream. The shops also have 'fresh cabinets' containing a selection of scrubs, masks and cleansers, and even a cleansing mask for men made with home-baked bread. See page 69 for our exclusive Lush bath soak recipe.

The renaissance in soapmaking as a cottage industry is particularly prevalent in the United States. In the UK, many individuals, and women in particular, are setting up satellite companies, often selling their products direct at craft fairs and wholesale to specialist stores. Considerable care and creativity is demonstrated by these people, both in the use of fine ingredients and the decoration and presentation of their soaps. These enterprises have, in fact, challenged many of the larger soap manufacturers to package their products as wholesome lookalikes. Yet, in reality, some of these 'natural' soaps are made using the same processes and ingredients as the mass-market polished bars that are so familiar to us, so you should be selective about what you buy.

What is clear is that the soap industry in general has always been initiated on sound principles and good intentions. Soapmakers of the 1990s are a sharing community and perhaps this attitude will, in addition to cleanliness, take us a little nearer to that much sought-after 'godliness'.

basic know-how

The product that we know of as soap is the result of mixing an acid with a caustic alkali. Most methods of soapmaking use vegetable or animal fats and oils as the acid, and sodium hydroxide (caustic soda/lye) as the alkali. When the alkali is diluted with water and added to the acid, a reaction called 'saponification' occurs. Once this has happened the alkali is on its way to being neutralized and, after curing the soap for several weeks, it should no longer be in evidence. Soap, therefore, is made with sodium hydroxide but does not contain it.

Saponification is an easy stage to recognize but the time it takes depends on a large number of variables, including the temperature of your mixture and the specific fats that you are using (see Basic Oils and Fats on pages 14-16). When saponification occurs your soap thickens to a point referred to by soapmakers as 'trace'. To establish whether you have reached trace, spoon some soap from the pot and then dribble it back over the surface of the mixture. If the dribble sits on top of the mixture, forming a raised line, you have reached trace. While trace can occur in as short a time as 5 minutes, do not worry if it takes several hours. Unless you have made big mistakes with your weights and measures, the soap will trace eventually.

Colourings, fragrances and fillers are all added as the mixture reaches trace and the soap is then poured into moulds, covered with a blanket or towel for insulation and left to set.

weights & measures

The success or failure of your batch of soap relies, above all, on one crucial factor: correct proportions of ingredients. If you wish to add to or alter the ingredients, read the Saponification Chart on page 17 for guidance on how to do this. The majority of recipes in this book will provide you with 2-lb (900-g) batches; depending on the moulds you select, these should result in 10-14 average-sized bars of soap.

Please note that, with the exception of spoonfuls and drops of ingredients, all quantities listed in the recipes are weighed quantities, so where water is quoted in ounces, these are weighed ounces and not fluid ounces. To weigh ingredients like this, place your chosen empty container on the scales and turn the setting back to zero. Then add your ingredients to the container until the weight reads as specified in the recipe. Use either ounces or grams, but do not mix the two in a recipe.

techniques

There are various ways that trace times can be reduced. Whisking the soap with a stainless steel whisk will speed up the process, as will the use of a hand-held electric mixer. If, however, you are going to use one of these miracles of modern science please ensure that the speed control is set at low before placing it in your soap pot. This warning comes from someone who, with the speed control set at 3, turned on her mixer and plastered the whole room (and herself) with flying, caustic soap.

Another shortcut is to place your soap pot in a warm oven (at the lowest setting), although personally, I find that the old-fashioned look-and-stir approach is preferable because it means that you will not miss trace and find that your soap has solidified in the pot.

setting times

Once again, these are dependent on a number of factors, including ingredients, room temperature and so on. However, on average, your soap should be hard enough to remove from the moulds 24-48 hours after pouring. Soaps based on vegetable oils take longer to harden than those made with meat fats. It is important to unmould the soap as soon as it reaches the consistency of hard cheese. At this stage you will be able to cut it into bars with ease.

curing

Stack the cut soap in a well-ventilated room and cover it with blankets to continue the curing process. During this process any residual sodium hydroxide is neutralized, which can result in changes to the appearance of your soap. A fine white dust, or even a crust, may appear on the surface of the soap. This is soda ash and can be scraped or even washed off the soap once the curing process is complete. It may help to wrap the soap in clingfilm directly after it has been poured into the mould.

You will also find that your soap will shrink during the curing process and, for this reason, it is wise not to attach ball-bands until the soap has completely settled. Some colourings will also fade – to reduce this possibility, turn the soap regularly so that all sides receive equal exposure to the light during the curing process.

In this book we use the cold-process method of soapmaking. This ensures that glycerine, which is a valuable by-product of the saponification process, remains in the finished soap, whereas in commercial soapmaking this is often extracted and sold separately.

acidity

You may be aware and concerned about the term 'pH balance', which measures acidity. Most cold-process soaps have a pH balance of about 9, although soapers aim to reduce this to 7 or 8 (just above neutral). The pH of your soap will reduce during the curing process but it is extremely difficult to control without the use of harsh chemicals which are, in effect, worse for your skin than a soap with a high pH content.

While the ingredients in the soaps in this book make them mild and gentle, if you are concerned you can test the pH of your soap with papers that can be purchased from aquarium shops, school suppliers and chemical laboratories. If a soap reads above 10, don't throw it away – use it for the laundry or rebatch it (see page 18).

materials & equipment

One of the great delights of soapmaking is that nearly all the equipment you need can be found in the average kitchen. Provided you wash this equipment in normal dishwashing liquid after soapmaking, there is no need to set aside special pots, pans and utensils specifically for your new addiction. Check that you have the following:

ASSORTED PLASTIC CONTAINERS: You can use these as moulds (see page 12).

DROPPER: This is optional, but it is useful when adding diluted pigments.

EYE PROTECTION: Wear a large pair of spectacles or plastic protective goggles, which can be bought in DIY stores.

HAND-HELD CHEESE-GRATER: Alternatively, use a food-processor. Either one is invaluable for rebatching (see page 18).

HAND-HELD POTATO-PEELER: Alternatively, you can use a cheese-slicer. Both are for trimming the soap.

KITCHEN SCALES: Ordinary kitchen scales will do fine (provided they are accurate) but if you are buying new ones invest in scales that you can manually turn back to zero. Postage scales are particularly useful for measuring the sodium hydroxide.

LARGE COOKING POT: This is your soap pot and should be made of either stainless steel or unchipped enamel. Do not use iron or aluminium as these will be affected by the sodium hydroxide (caustic soda/lye).

MEASURING JUG OR BOWL: Choose one in plastic or ovenproof glass. This will be used for weighing your water and for mixing your sodium hydroxide.

MEASURING SPOONS: Choose a selection in various sizes to use with the colourants.

NON-STICK COOKING SPRAY: This is used for greasing your moulds. Solid vegetable fat will also do.

OLD BLANKETS OR TOWELS: These are used to insulate your finished soap.

PLASTIC SPATULAS: You will need two. These are for stirring your soapmix and your sodium hydroxide and for scraping the sides of your soap pot.

RUBBER GLOVES: These are essential protection from the caustic ingredients in the soap. Regularly check for holes.

SHARP KNIFE: You need this to cut the soap into bars.

SODIUM HYDROXIDE (CAUSTIC SODA/LYE): This can be purchased from chemist's shops or plumber's supply merchants. Make sure that the brand you buy contains a high percentage of sodium hydroxide. Keep it in an airtight container and handle with extreme care. If the granules are exposed to damp they will solidify into hard lumps, although they are still usable like this.

SPONGES OR DISHCLOTHS: You need these for mopping up spilt soap. Remember that newly-made soap is caustic, so rinse the sponges and cloths thoroughly after use.

STAINLESS STEEL LADLE: When making large batches of soap you may find it easier to ladle rather than pour the mixture into the moulds.

SUGAR THERMOMETERS: You will need two. Buy glass, not aluminium, thermometers that register from below 100°F (38°C) and up to at least 200°F (93°C).

shapes & sizes

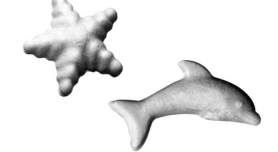

One of the first things you will discover as a truly addicted soapmaker is that, when shopping, packaging becomes far more important than product. No longer will you select your meat, fruit and dairy items on the basis of quality, you will now buy them because they are sitting in wonderfully moulded plastic packs. Your refrigerator will be full of prettily shaped but inedible mousses and yoghurts in weird and wonderful flavours, and those fancy rubber ice trays and butter moulds will be firmly designated to the soapmaking cupboard.

A visit to a DIY store will gain new meaning. PVC pipes, guttering and the lengths of rectangular plastic conduits (used to hide electric wiring) all make wonderful soap moulds, as do children's hollow rubber toys, drawer-dividers, plastic storage boxes, plastic microwave dishes

and even the cardboard trays that hold tins of cat food in the supermarket. The rule is this: if it's flexible plastic, clear polystyrene (with no holes in the bottom), cardboard or wood, and can be lined with dustbin liners, it will make the perfect soap mould.

Perhaps you prefer a more refined approach? Several companies produce trays of purpose-built soap moulds that will offer you a wide variety of fancy designs. See, for example, the angel shapes on page 56 and the seashore shapes above. You can also buy plastic moulds designed for candlemaking and latex moulds commonly used for model-making. If, however, you are intending to use a finely detailed mould, it is wise to work with a hard-finish or a glycerine soap to ensure that none of the details chip off during the removal process.

In addition to moulds, slabs of soap, moulded in shallow boxes, can be stamped out with fancy biscuit-cutters to create serrated circles, squares, stars and heart shapes. You can also cut larger blocks into hexagonals, oblongs, cubes or whatever your heart desires.

When choosing and using a mould, there are a few hints and tips that will help you to produce a perfect result.

1 When lining a cardboard box with a dustbin liner, take care to eliminate as many creases as possible because these will appear on the surface of your finished soap.

2 When using a PVC pipe, cut it into 12-in (30-cm) lengths and cap one end with a circle of plastic or card taped very firmly to the pipe. Stand the pipe in a bucket or jug before pouring in the fresh soap, just in case the tape isn't as strong as you thought it was. Once the soap has

set, remove the circle of plastic or card and place the pipe in the freezer for a couple of hours. Remove it and allow slight condensation to form. Cut out a round disc of plastic or heavyweight card slightly smaller than the diameter of your pipe. Place this over the soap at one end of the pipe and then push the soap through to the other end with a stick. (This might take two people.) Alternatively, make a split down the length of the pipe and cover with strong, plastic adhesive tape. Remove the tape after the soap has set and ease open the split before pushing the soap through the pipe as previously described.

3 Do not use aluminium cookie trays as these will corrode and the aluminium will come off on your soap.

4 Always grease plastic and rubber moulds before use with either solid vegetable fat or a non-stick cooking spray.

5 It is sometimes difficult to remove soap from rigid plastic moulds. One solution is to place the soap-filled mould in the freezer and leave it for several hours. Once removed, let it stand until condensation forms – the soap should then pop out of the mould with ease.

6 Purpose-built moulds usually produce small, flat-based shapes of soap but, in some instances (depending on the shape), you can stick the soaps back to back to create a solid and larger bar. Use fresh, wet soap as a glue for this purpose.

cutting your soap

After the soap has set it will cut in a similar way to cheese, and a flat-bladed kitchen knife or a cheese-wire should allow you to do this with ease. If you have made a flat tray of soap, score cut lines in the surface to determine the size of your bars before cutting right through.

I sometimes use an empty pack of 20 cigarettes as a template for this because it is a comfortable size for a bar of soap. Keep your knife level as you cut, then square up any uneven edges or surfaces with a vegetable knife or peeler. Flat surfaces can also be levelled off with a cheese-slicer.

the ten commandments

Many people express concern about the dangers of using sodium hydroxide (caustic soda/lye) and, indeed, it is certainly necessary to take basic safety precautions when handling it. However, all that is required is a little common sense, which you already have or you wouldn't have bought this book. Take note of the following ten commandments and nothing untoward will happen to you.

1 Store sodium hydroxide (caustic soda/lye) in an airtight container on a high shelf. Clearly label the container and do not, under any circumstances, leave it accessible to children, poodles that don't mind their own business or curious cats.

2 Always wear rubber gloves when handling sodium hydroxide, mixing soap and unmoulding fresh soap.

3 Wear eye-goggles or large glasses when handling or mixing sodium hydroxide solution with fats. If your partner/children ask you why you are wearing them, say you are going to audition as a Dame Edna Everage lookalike.

4 Do not touch the sodium hydroxide with rubber gloves and then rub your eyes – that would be pretty dumb and don't ask me how I know …

5 As you add the water to the sodium hydroxide, choking fumes will rise from the bowl. Keep your face well away from these fumes as you stir the mixture or, better still, tie a scarf around your nose and pretend to be a bank robber. Don't worry, these fumes will only last for a few moments. Even so, always work in a well-ventilated area.

6 Do not leave the sodium hydroxide or soap mixtures unlidded and unattended. If you need the bathroom, cross your legs. That sort of accident is preferable to the kind that can happen to pets and children if they get near the mixtures.

7 Don't mistake your soap mixture for cake mixture or soup – it doesn't taste as good as it looks.

8 Tempting though it will most definitely be, don't sample your soap before the four-week deadline is up. If you are pathetically weak-willed you may wash your hands while wearing rubber gloves just to see the bubbles.

9 When making soap, keep a bottle of vinegar next to the sink. If accidental splashes occur, immediately wash the affected area with the vinegar and then rinse with water. Splashes in the eyes need medical treatment. As an immediate remedy, douse them continually with cold water.

10 When cleaning your soap pot, let the mixture harden and then scrape the remains into a plastic bag which should be sealed and put in the rubbish. Add vinegar to your washing up water and wash the utensils as normal (wearing a pair of rubber gloves) with dishwashing liquid.

basic oils & fats

Soap can be made from virtually any combination of oils and fats, but your choice should depend on the qualities you want from a finished bar. Some oils offer large bubbles, others a creamy texture. Some combinations are good for greasy skin, others for dry or normal skin. The oil you choose will also affect the time the soap takes to trace and the consistency of the finished bar.

It seems reasonable to believe that if you don't have one fat or oil in your cupboard you can substitute another. Wrong! The amount of sodium hydroxide (caustic soda/lye) needed to saponify a particular fat or oil differs considerably and if the wrong amount is used you could end up with a very harsh or very sloppy bar of soap sitting on your sink top. If you want to substitute oils, turn to page 16 where a simple formula is provided that will enable you to do this successfully. The list below gives some of the more popular oils and fats and describes their characteristics.

popular oils & fats

ALMOND OIL: This wonderful oil is used widely in cosmetics and its inclusion in soap makes for a hard bar and lovely soft skin. I use it both as a base oil and for superfatting (see page 16). Almond oil is rich in protein and offers relief for itchy or inflamed skin.

BEEF FAT/TALLOW/DRIPPING: In the UK it is possible to buy refined beef fat (sold as dripping) in most supermarkets. In other countries it is necessary to render down fat straight from the butcher's shop and this, speaking personally, rather reduces the sensual delights of soapmaking. That aside, the use of beef fat results in a lovely hard, mild bar of soap. It traces reasonably quickly and produces a white soap which is a good base for colourings. Bubbles are small but the bars are long-lasting.

CASTOR OIL: This oil is extracted from the seed of the castor bean plant and can be bought in pharmacies. With the exception of its use in glycerine soap it is rarely included in large quantities within a batch. Castor oil has

tremendous moisturizing qualities and is used most successfully for superfatting purposes (see page 16).

COCONUT OIL: This is the number one oil for soapmakers, although when used on its own it can tend to dry the skin. It is available from Indian grocery stores and US popcorn manufacturers. Coconut oil produces a hard soap with large, creamy bubbles.

LARD: This provides an accessible and cheap base for soapmakers. It also has the advantage of producing a white bar of soap with large bubbles.

OLIVE OIL: Packed with vitamins, minerals and proteins, any grade of olive oil can be used in soapmaking. It also provides an excellent base for infused herbal oils (see pages 20-21). Olive oil produces a mild, creamy soap with small bubbles but good emollient qualities. It is excellent for shampoo bars and for baby soaps.

PALM OIL: Not easily obtainable in the UK but well worth seeking out as a mild, basic oil. Palm oil produces a creamy soap with small bubbles that clean well. Many commercial soaps use palm oil as a base but it is used to best advantage in combination with coconut or olive oil. It traces quickly and makes a hard, long-lasting bar of soap.

SHORTENING/VEGETABLE FATS/OILS: Most brands sold in the UK contain a combination of rapeseed, soybean and sometimes sunflower oils. These can vary within a brand depending on availability. These blended oils tend to result in soft bars of soap but, when combined with other oils and fats, provide a cheap base for a satisfactory end result. They are a good alternative to dripping for those who prefer not to use animal fats.

SUNFLOWER OIL: Pressed from sunflower seeds, this wholesome oil is widely available, inexpensive and full of vitamins and minerals. It is best used in combination with coconut oil or dripping as it tends to result in a soft soap and is slow to trace. It is good for all skin types and produces medium-sized bubbles.

precious additives

The following additives are included to give your soap character, texture and skin-pampering qualities. Some are expensive to buy but the difference to your soap will be evident even when only small quantities are included – approximately 1 tbsp (15g) per lb (454g) soap. These are the ingredients you play with once you have produced several successful batches of basic soap and are truly hooked on the sensual pleasures that only a handmade bar of soap can provide.

Look out, too, for the preservatives in this list, which should be used whenever you add an ingredient with a short shelf-life, such as fresh fruit. Unless stated otherwise, these gems should be added the moment that your soap traces so that the possibility of the sodium hydroxide eating

up their qualities will be diminished. More additives appear in the Fillers section (see pages 24-25).

ALOE VERA GEL: Extracted from the leaf of a cactus, this is a healing gel which is good for dry or chapped skin, eczema and burns.

APRICOT KERNEL OIL: This contains skin-softening properties, vitamins and minerals. Good for skin that has aged prematurely and for sensitive skins.

AVOCADO OIL: This contains vitamins, protein, lecithin and fatty acids, all of which are especially beneficial for those with dry skin or eczema.

BEESWAX: White beeswax pellets are used widely in cosmetics as an emulsifier. The rich gold variety will give your soap a honey smell and a waxy feel. It will also speed up trace. Saponify this with your base oils and use approximately 1oz (28g) per lb (454g) of soap.

BENZOIN: This is a resin available either powdered or as a tincture. It has a terrific scent in its own right but also acts as a fragrance fixative.

CARROT ROOT OIL: An antioxidant rich in vitamins A and C. It is especially good for dry and chapped skin.

COCOA BUTTER: This looks and smells like white chocolate and contributes to the hardness of your soap. It has wonderful soothing and emollient qualities. It is widely used as a base in cosmetics.

EVENING PRIMROSE OIL: Good for eczema and helps to prevent premature ageing of the skin.

GLYCERINE: A clear, syrupy liquid available from pharmacies. Although your soap already contains glycerine, extra can be added at trace to increase its moisturizing qualities.

GRAPEFRUIT SEED EXTRACT (GSE): This is a valuable antioxidant with antibacterial and deodorizing properties. One teaspoonful (5g) added to a 2-lb (908-g) batch of oils (before the sodium hydroxide is added) will speed up trace time considerably.

both petroleum jelly (Vaseline) and mineral oil (baby oil) are derivatives of the petroleum industry. While these are widely used in cosmetics, given their origins some people may wish to avoid them. tip

HONEY: This has wonderful emollient properties but is best added with beeswax because it tends to soften soap when used on its own.

JOJOBA OIL: Great in shampoo bars, jojoba oil is both a moisturizer and a humectant. Widely used in cosmetics, this is a costly but valuable additive to soap.

KUKUI NUT OIL: Originating in Hawaii, this oil is high in essential fatty acids and is particularly soothing for sunburnt and chapped skin.

LANOLIN: Beware, because some people are allergic to this wax which comes from sheep's wool. For those who are not, lanolin has great skin-softening properties.

MILK: Use fresh goats' milk as a replacement for water to create a soothing, creamy bar of soap. Dried cows' milk can also be added at trace as an alternative.

MUSTARD POWDER: A small quantity of mustard powder can be added to soaps to open and unclog pores.

ROSEHIP SEED OIL: A natural preservative, high in essential fatty acids. It eases inflammation and acts as a moisturizer. It is a good additive to shampoo bars for delicate hair.

SHEA BUTTER: This moisturizing and nourishing butter will not saponify and so remains in your soap to soothe sensitive skins.

VITAMIN E OIL: This is an antioxidant that retards deterioration of fresh matter in soap. It also prevents skin wrinkles.

WHEATGERM OIL: This is an emollient and an antioxidant that is particularly gentle. It is a good additive for facial soaps.

saponification chart

Each oil that you choose for your soapmaking requires a specific amount of sodium hydroxide (caustic soda/lye) to create the reaction called saponification that transforms it into soap. This is one area of soapmaking that calls for absolute precision since if excess sodium hydroxide remains in your soap it can irritate and burn the skin. Large excesses of fat will result in a soft, soggy soap that could turn rancid.

superfatting

One exception to the rule of precision is a technique known as superfatting. Here, an excess of up to 5 per cent of the total oils and fats in your soap can be added to your mixture. Usually, these are oils of special value, such as avocado, apricot or wheatgerm. When added at trace, these will not fully saponify and their therapeutic value will therefore remain relatively unaffected by the caustic solution.

The following chart will enable you to calculate exactly how much sodium hydroxide you require to saponify your base oils and fats. It was produced by Elaine White, the US 'Soap Starlet', and I am extremely indebted to her for allowing me to share it with you.

The calculation is very simple. If you are working in ounces, multiply the number of ounces by the figure listed on the chart. For example, 16oz of olive oil requires 16 x 0.134 (the number for olive oil), which equals 2.1oz.

Round this up or down to the nearest $\frac{1}{4}$ of an ounce and that is the amount of sodium hydroxide required to saponify 1lb of olive oil. If you are working in grams, divide the number of grams by 28.35 to convert it to ounces before you do the sodium hydroxide calculation. Then multiply the result by 28.35 to convert it back to grams.

In addition to this canny piece of mathematical wizardry, a spreadsheet program, created by Theresa Lott, is available on the Internet. This will do the calculations for you and enable you to translate your grams to ounces and ounces to grams. Theresa offers this program free to soaplist members (see page 79).

saponification chart

0.136	almond oil, sweet almond oil, *Prunus amygdalus* oil
0.135	apricot kernel oil, *Prunus armeniaca* oil
0.136	arachis oil, peanut oil, earthnut oil, katchung oil
0.133	avocado oil, *Persea americana* oil
0.175	babassu, Brazil nut oil
0.069	bayberry or myrtle wax
0.140	beef tallow, beef fat, beef suet, dripping
0.069	beeswax
0.136	borage oil, *Borago officinalis* oil
0.175	Brazil nut oil, babassu oil
0.124	canola oil, rapeseed oil, colza oil, rape oil, ramic oil
0.069	carnauba wax
0.128	castor oil, ricinus oil
0.138	chicken fat
0.137	cocoa butter
0.190	coconut oil, *Cocos nucifera* oil
0.132	cod liver oil
0.136	corn oil, maize oil
0.138	cottonseed oil
0.139	deer tallow, venison fat
0.136	evening primrose oil, *Oenothera biennis* oil
0.135	flax seed oil
0.139	goat tallow, goat fat
0.136	goose fat
0.123 to 0.135	grape seed oil, grapefruit seed oil, *Vitis vinifera* oil (varies widely)
0.136	hazelnut oil, *Corylus avellana* oil
0.137	hemp oil, hemp seed oil
0.136	herring oil, fish oil
0.137	java cotton, Kapok oil
0.069	jojoba oil
0.128	Karite butter, shea butter
0.135	kukui oil
0.074	lanolin, sheep wool fat
0.138	lard, pork tallow, pork fat

0.136	linseed oil, flax seed oil
0.139	macadamia nut oil, *Macadamia integrifolia* oil
0.136	margarine
0.140	mink oil
0.123	mustard seed oil
0.138	mutton tallow, sheep tallow
0.141	neat's foot oil, beef hoof oil
0.134	olive oil, loccu oil, Florence oil, olium olivate
0.156	palm kernel oil, palm butter
0.141	palm oil
0.136	peanut oil, earthnut oil
0.135	pistachio oil
0.138	poppy seed oil
0.135	pumpkin seed oil
0.128	rice bran oil
0.136	safflower oil
0.135	sardine oil, Japan fish oil
0.133	sesame seed oil, gigely oil
0.128	shea butter, African karite butter
0.138	sheep fat, sheep tallow
0.074	sheep wool fat, lanolin
0.136	shortening, vegetable shortening, hydrogenated vegetable oil
0.135	soybean oil, Chinese bean oil, *Helianthus annus* oil
0.134	sunflower seed oil
0.137	Theobroma oil, cocoa butter
0.137	tung oil, soybean oil, China wood oil, nut oil
0.138	venison fat, deer fat, deer or venison tallow
0.136	walnut oil, *Juglans regia* oil
0.138	whale: baleen whale
0.092	whale: sperm whale, body, blubber oil
0.102	whale: sperm whale, head
0.132	wheatgerm oil, *Triticum vulgare* oil
0.074	wool fat, lanolin

rebatching & recycling

There is no need to throw away your soap if something goes wrong with it or you don't like the results. Instead, you can reprocess or recycle it. You can also reconstitute soap that you've made.

rebatching soap

This is the term used for reconstituting cured and part-cured soap. This technique offers several major advantages. Firstly, it greatly reduces the possibility of the sodium hydroxide (caustic soda/lye) in your soap distorting the colourings and fragrances. Secondly, it allows you to recycle trimmings and misshapen soaps, thereby totally eliminating waste. Brighter colours can be achieved and fragrances will last longer when added to a rebatch, and you can also add fresh herbs and flower petals with less risk of them becoming discoloured. Rebatched soaps can be poured into fancy moulds because you are not limited to using the plastic, glass or stainless steel moulds required for a batch of soap made from scratch.

Rebatching is quite a simple procedure, although some soapers do seem to find it difficult to achieve a creamy, pourable soap that is free from what look like lumps of mashed potato. However, the following method has always served me well and I am confident that it will produce good results for you.

1 Make your basic soap in the normal way and set it aside until it is good and hard. Many soapers find that soaps made from animal fats give better results in a rebatch than soaps made from vegetable fats. If you prefer to use a vegetable-based soap, leave it to cure for at least three weeks before rebatching.

2 Using the smallest holes on a cheese-grater, an electric food-processor or an old-fashioned mincer, grind the soap into the finest consistency you can achieve.

3 Weigh the ground soap. Set aside 12oz (340g) warm, distilled or spring water for every lb (454g) of soap.

4 Place the ground soap and three-quarters of the water in a double-boiler (or in a bowl placed in a saucepan half-full of water) over a medium heat and stir until all the soap is wet. Add the remaining water and stir again.

5 Cover the pot with a lid or a piece of foil and leave it to simmer. The melting-down process can take up to 1 hour and the soap should be stirred intermittently until all the lumps have dissolved.

6 When the soap has reached a smooth, creamy consistency, remove it from the heat and add your colouring, fragrance and/or fillers, stirring until they are evenly distributed. The consistency of the soap mix may change on adding the fragrance oils. If it thins, keep stirring until it is smooth and creamy. If it thickens, add more water and stir rapidly.

7 Continue to stir until the mixture cools, then pour it into pre-greased moulds and leave to set as normal.

recycling soap

Follow the rebatching procedure when recycling soap leftovers. These may contain many different colours and textures, so you will never create a pure white soap or a flat, creamy bar. Use your recycling batches for herbal or oatmeal soaps where texture is a feature. Try replacing the water with goats' milk or half-water, half-goats' milk, to create a nice, rich soap. You can experiment with layering too - melt down small amounts of soap and add different colourings to each batch.

tip

t ry making a soap that floats! Whisk the soap mixture briskly with a stainless steel whisk before pouring your rebatch into moulds. If the soap is going to float, it must be the consistency of whipped cream before you pour it.

One of the most delightful aspects of making your own soap is choosing the fragrance. Before you do this, you have to consider a number of elements. Firstly, what is the purpose of the soap? In other words, is the batch designed for sensual languishing, brutal scrubbing, cleaning and deodorizing, or perhaps healing a sensitive skin? Do you want a fresh, crisp scent or a musky, spicy fragrance? Do you crave the sweetness of morning dew or a whiff of the Orient? All the above, and more, can be achieved by combining a selection of essential oils. Have fun experimenting.

scent stability

The second consideration is the stability of the essential oil that you choose. Some oils stand up better to the saponification process than others and several, particularly those within the citrus group, require a fixative such as benzoin, vitamin E or tea tree oil to be added to the batch.

what are essential oils?

Essential oils are plant extracts, usually obtained by distillation. Large amounts of plant matter are required to produce minute amounts of oil, and this accounts for their considerable price. Essential oils are powerful stuff and should be treated with the same respect as chemicals. Always mix an essential oil with a base oil, such as almond oil, before applying directly to the skin, and wear rubber gloves when handling it. Do not use essential oils if you suffer from skin allergies or if you are in the first four months of pregnancy. If neat oil is accidentally splashed or rubbed in your eyes, immediately flush them with milk or clean, warm water. Spilt essential oils can also remove varnish and paint from furniture so, if you have an accident, wash the surfaces immediately with a sponge and warm, soapy water.

healing properties

Aromatherapists will tell you of the healing properties of many essential oils. While it is debatable whether or not the saponification process kills these qualities, it is certainly true that fragrances can create or alter a mood, and my advice would be to select essential oils on the assumption that their healing properties will be retained in the finished bar.

fragrant alternatives

Essential oils can be extremely costly and a workable alternative is the range of synthetic fragrance oils that are often cunningly packaged to resemble their essential cousins. You will be able to spot the difference between the two firstly by the price and secondly by the warning notice, in the small print, which tells you not to use the oils on the skin. While this warning should certainly be heeded if you intend to market your soap, the minute quantities required in soap make fragrance oils quite safe, provided they are not intended for a particularly sensitive skin. The quality of fragrance oils varies considerably from scent to scent and from brand to brand. Be very choosy, particularly with floral fragrances, or you may end up with a bar of soap that smells like bathroom air-freshener.

Many soapers are tempted by the possibilities of creating their own essential oils but, in reality, the distillation process requires such large amounts of petals that the results are hardly worth it. A useful and simple alternative for the home soapmaker is to infuse a base oil with fresh flowers and herbs before adding it to your soap. To do this, crush your petals or herbs to release the scent and pack them loosely in a wide-necked bottle. Fill the bottle with olive, sunflower or almond oil and stir well.

Cover the bottle opening with muslin and place it in a sunny position (or a warm place), then leave for two weeks, shaking the bottle every day. Strain off the oil and refill the bottle with fresh plants. Repeat until the oil smells strongly of the flowers or herbs.

A similar process can be used with solid fats. Take coconut or vegetable fat and melt this in a saucepan filled with fresh petals or herbs. Stir continuously while the mixture cools. Re-melt the oils and drain off the petals, replacing these with a fresh batch. Repeat until the cooled fat smells strongly of the flowers or herbs.

It is also possible to infuse the water content of your soap in a similar way. Pour boiling water over a saucepan full of bruised petals or herbs and seal with a lid. Leave the flowers to infuse for two hours and then strain off the petals. Repeat until the water is strongly scented. By following this process you are creating a 'tea'. You can, of course, use commercial, herbal teabags to achieve a similar result.

troubleshooting

You should be aware that both essential and fragrance oils can cause your soap to curdle and, for this reason, it is wise to include them directly after trace, when the sodium hydroxide (caustic soda/lye) is at its weakest. Should your soap begin to curdle or seize, beat it rapidly with a stainless steel whisk and then pour immediately into the mould.

mixing scents

While many single essential oils will provide you with a delightful and recognizable fragrance, it is a gratifying experience to combine different oils and create your own personal, perfumed masterpiece. However, before doing this, it is important to understand the principal of the 'three notes'. Notes are the categories used to define the strength and substance of a specific scent. Oils in the top notes category are the first to reach your nose but can be fleeting; middle notes provide a solid centre to the fragrance; and base notes act as a fixative and are perhaps the most sensual of the combination. As a rule of thumb, oils with a middle note should make up about 70 per cent of the total mix.

Here is a list of some of the most popular essential oils and their qualities. I have not had the space to include all of them, so do check out the books in the bibliography (see page 79) for further reading on this fascinating subject.

BAY, WEST INDIAN (*PIMENTA RACEMOSA*) BASE NOTE: Widely used in perfumery, this rich, aromatic oil is particularly sensual when mixed with nutmeg and mandarin. It makes a great masculine soap.

BERGAMOT (*CITRUS BERGAMIA*) TOP NOTE: Produced from orange rind, this is a clean, fresh, revitalizing scent often used in aftershaves. Good for greasy skin and recommended by aromatherapists for the treatment of eczema and acne.

CAMOMILE, ROMAN (*ANTHEMIS NOBILIS*) TOP NOTE:
Distilled from the flowers and leaves of this common herb, camomile is good for dry and sensitive skins and recommended by aromatherapists to relieve acne and dermatitis. Great for facial soaps and steam baths, with a clean, fresh scent.

CARDAMOM (*ELLETARIA CARDAMOMUM*) TOP NOTE:
Exotic, spicy scent extracted from the plant seed. Relieves headaches and nausea.

CARROT (*DAUCUS CAROTA*) MIDDLE NOTE: This has a revitalizing scent. It is particularly good for sensitive skins and is recommended by aromatherapists for the treatment of eczema and psoriasis.

CEDARWOOD (*CEDRUS ATLANTICA*) BASE NOTE:
Extracted from the wood of the cedar tree, cedarwood provides a soft, woody undertone that calms anxiety, especially when blended with sandalwood. Good antiseptic properties.

CITRONELLA (*CYMBOPOGON NARDUS*) TOP NOTE:
Refreshing citrus fragrance, extremely useful as a bug repellent and deodorant. Include citronella in dog shampoo bars to reduce the possibility of fleas.

CLARY SAGE (*SALVIA SCLAREA*) MIDDLE NOTE:
Extracted from the flowers of the herb, this is the scent to use if you love the smell of a country morning. This precious oil has antiseptic and deodorizing qualities.

EUCALYPTUS (*EUCALYPTUS GLOBULUS*) TOP NOTE:
Powerful, antiseptic scent. Useful as an insect/flea repellent and recommended by aromatherapists for relief from acne. Anti-fungal and a good ingredient for hand soaps.

FRANKINCENSE (*BOSWELLIA CARTERI*) BASE NOTE:
Exotic, spicy, balsamic fragrance with antiseptic and revitalizing qualities. Good for ageing, oily or cracked skins. Use in a facial steam bath or lotion.

GERANIUM (*PELARGONIUM ROSEUM*) MIDDLE NOTE:
Sweet, heady fragrance which benefits from combination with the sharper citrus or lavender oils. Anti-depressant qualities, good for all skin types and recommended by aromatherapists for relief from eczema and dermatitis. Good ingredient for skin lotions.

GINGER (*ZINGIBER OFFICINALE*) MIDDLE NOTE: Warm, spicy fragrance with antiseptic qualities. Good addition to masculine soaps.

GRAPEFRUIT (*CITRUS X PARADISI*): See lemon.

HOWOOD LEAF (*CINNAMOMUM CAMPHORA*):
See rosewood.

LAVENDER (*LAVANDULA OFFICINALIS*) TOP NOTE: Fresh, pungent fragrance with antiseptic and antibiotic qualities. Recommended for greasy and sensitive skin types. Also useful as an insect repellent.

LEMON (*CITRUS LIMONUM*) TOP NOTE: Clear, strong fragrance that needs stabilizing in soap with a fixative such as benzoin. Good for greasy skins with anti-fungal and astringent qualities. Combine with a rough filler to exfoliate the skin.

MANDARIN (*CITRUS RETICULATA*): See tangerine.

MARJORAM (*ORIGANUM MARJORANA*) TOP NOTE: Extracted from the flowers of the herb, a warm, leafy scent that blends well with lavender and citrus oils. Good for greasy skins due to its antiseptic qualities. Add this one to a footbath.

MYRRH (*COMMIPHORA MYRRHA*) BASE NOTE: Warm and woody and good for the fingernails.

NEROLI (*MELALEUCA VIRIDIFLORA*) MIDDLE NOTE: Distilled from the blossom of the bitter orange tree, this pungent, sweet scent forms the basis of eau de Cologne. It has revitalizing properties and is recommended by aromatherapists for the relief of dermatitis.

PATCHOULI (*POGOSTEMON PATCHOULI*) BASE NOTE: Love it or loathe it, this is the oil of the 1960s when it saturated the incense sticks of every self-respecting hippy. A warm, peppery fragrance, patchouli has antiseptic qualities and is recommended for the relief of acne and eczema. It also combats dandruff, so consider it for use in your shampoo bars.

PEPPERMINT (*MENTHA PIPERITA*) TOP NOTE: Clean, fresh and a little overpowering, peppermint is best used alone. It has antiseptic and insect-repellent qualities. Soap made with stimulating peppermint is a good choice for the morning after the night before.

PINE (*PINUS SYLVESTRIS*) MIDDLE NOTE: A classic soaper's scent, the fresh smell of pine helps the circulation and keeps the flies away. Ideal fragrance for the men in your life.

ROSE OTTO (*ROSA DAMASCENA*) MIDDLE NOTE: This very precious oil is wasted in soap. While its heady scent is seductive and its antiseptic qualities are useful, shock at the price of the stuff could eliminate the anti-stress/depressant qualities it is said to contain. Try a rose fragrance oil instead.

ROSEWOOD (*ANIBA PARVIFLORA*) MIDDLE NOTE: This sweet, spicy scent is distilled from a hardwood tree and its use is therefore environmentally unfriendly. Howood leaf is said to be a good, friendly alternative. Rosewood stimulates the skin cells and tissues and is beneficial to ageing skins. It is also an aphrodisiac, which probably explains why I have been politically incorrect and included it here.

SANDALWOOD (*SANTALUM ALBUM*) BASE NOTE: Warm, woody fragrance with antiseptic and astringent qualities, sandalwood is good for dry and ageing skin and is recommended by aromatherapists for relief from eczema and skin irritations.

TANGERINE (*CITRUS RETICULATA*) MIDDLE NOTE: Sweet, tangy scent with antiseptic and soothing qualities, tangerine is a good choice for facial oils and lotions. When using it in soap, stabilize the scent with benzoin.

TEA TREE (*MELALEUCA ALTERNIFOLIA*) TOP NOTE: A thoroughly useful oil with a medicinal scent, tea tree acts as a preservative in soap. Strong antiseptic and cleansing qualities and helpful for itchy skin, insect bites and acne.

VANILLA (*VANILLA PLANIFOLIA*) BASE NOTE: Warm and welcoming oil with little to recommend it except its ability to make you constantly want to sniff (or lick) your bar of soap. Its inclusion also turns your soap dark brown.

YLANG-YLANG (*CANANGA ODORATA*) MIDDLE NOTE: A sweet, heady scent that is beautiful on its own and also blends well with clary sage. Good for most skin types, and particularly useful in shampoo bars and hair rinses because it acts as a tonic and promotes hair growth.

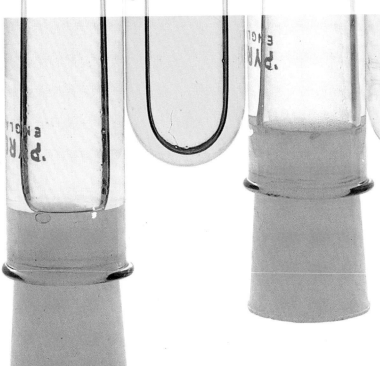

fillers are ingredients added to soap which have no effect on the saponification process. However, there are four good reasons for using them. The first is the beneficial effect of the specific filler on your skin. The second is economy (fillers increase the size of your final batch), the third is the visual pleasure of texture, and the fourth reason is the sheer delight of knowing that you are washing with, for example, fresh strawberries, cucumber or almonds. Dry fillers should be added to the soap mixture at trace (see Basic Know-how on pages 8-9), while wet fillers (fruit and vegetables) should be liquidized and used as a part substitute for the water content.

ALMONDS (GROUND): Ground almonds are frequently used in cosmetics as they help to unplug pores and exfoliate the skin. Only a teaspoonful (5g) per lb (454g) of soap is required to leave your skin silky soft and free from oil. If you can't stretch to the high price of ground almonds, try hazelnuts as an alternative. Blanch and then grind them to a fine powder before adding them to your soap.

APRICOTS: Dried or fresh apricots can be pulped and added to your soap but follow the general guidelines listed under Fruit and Vegetables below. Apricots are packed with vitamins and minerals and can act as a skin softener.

BORAX: This mineral increases the cleaning power of your soap, softens the water and acts as a valuable disinfectant. Use only one teaspoonful (5g) of borax powder per lb (454g) of soap. If you use more than this you may have problems with the texture of your soap.

BRAN: This is the outer husk of any grain and will add bulk and texture to your soap. It acts as a natural exfoliant as it is slightly abrasive. Add about 2 tablespoonfuls (10g) per pound (454g) of soap.

CARROTS: Also available as an essential oil, carrots can be liquidized and added directly to soap (see Fruit and Vegetables below). Rich in vitamins A and C, they are particularly good for chapped and dry skin.

CLAY (FRENCH): This is available in pink, grey and green and is also known as bentonite. It is useful for drawing toxins and dirt from the skin and gives your soap a smooth finish. Not recommended for dry skin, French clay can be purchased at health food and artists' supply shops. Use approximately 1 tablespoonful (15g) per lb (454g) of soap.

COFFEE: Fresh coffee beans, ground to a fine powder, are particularly useful for removing odours such as onion and garlic from your hands. Use approximately half a cup of grounds per lb (454g) of soap.

CORNMEAL: In addition to adding bulk to your batch, cornmeal is a useful exfoliant for greasy skin. Add 1 tablespoonful (15g) per lb (454g) of soap.

CUCUMBER: Often used in face packs, cucumbers have an astringent quality and good cleansing power. They should be liquidized before use (see Fruit and Vegetables below).

FLOWER PETALS: Dried flower petals can be ground up and added to your soap at trace. Rose and lavender both have astringent qualities, while calendula (pot marigold) is good for rough or cracked skin. Ground petals will discolour in soap but when used with an appropriate essential oil they act as a desirable additive and produce a speckled effect. Use about 2 tablespoonfuls (30g) per lb (454g) soap.

FRUIT AND VEGETABLES: Fresh fruit and vegetables can be liquidized and used as part of the water weight quoted in the individual recipes. They have no decorative element as they tend to turn brown when used in soap. They also reduce the life of the soap as saponification does not protect fresh produce from perishing. When including fruit and vegetables it is a good idea to add a teaspoon (5g) of grapefruit seed extract, carrot root oil, wheatgerm oil or powdered benzoin to your soap mix. These are all natural preservatives that will prolong the life of your soap. Many of the problems can be minimized by adding the fruit or vegetable element only to the water content of rebatched soap (see page 18). This way, it does not come into direct contact with the sodium hydroxide (caustic soda/lye).

FULLER'S EARTH: This is a brown clay which is particularly good for cleansing and removing dead cells from the skin. Its addition to soap produces a dense, heavy quality and it is best suited to oily or normal skin types. Use approximately 1 tablespoon (5g) per lb (454g) soap.

HAZELNUTS (GROUND): See almonds.

HERBS: Herbs should be dried and powdered before use and added at a ratio of 2 tablespoons (30g) per lb (454g) of soap. Dried herbs not only add texture and a decorative, 'country feel' to the finished soap, but they also have their own individual skincare properties which are discussed in the essential oils section of this book (see pages 21–23). If you wish to capture the quality of fresh herbs, infuse them in olive oil (see pages 20-21). While the leaves themselves will not be included in your soap, the therapeutic benefits, scent and colour of the herbs will be retained in the oil.

KAOLIN (WHITE CLAY): This is a pure white powder with astringent and cleansing properties. Use approximately 1 tablespoon (15g) per lb (454g) of soap. Not recommended for dry skin. Pure powdered kaolin can be bought in chemists and artists' supply shops.

LEMONS AND ORANGES: The dried and finely grated peel of citrus fruits contain a high level of vitamin C and is a valuable additive to soaps. Lemons, in particular, have strong anti-bacterial qualities, although the essential oils of the same fruits are notoriously difficult to use in soap and seldom retain their scent. Use approximately 1 tablespoon (15g) of powdered peel per lb (454g) of soap. Lemon juice can also be used as a part substitute for water.

OATMEAL: This will add pleasing texture to your soap and act as a gentle exfoliant. Use baby oatmeal or rolled oats ground with a food processor. Add approximately half a cup of oats per lb (454g) of soap for maximum usage.

PUMICE: The abrasive quality of finely-ground pumice will help to remove stubborn dirt and stains from the hands. Add approximately 2 tablespoons (30g) to every lb of soap. If you want to make your own pumice stones, add 4oz (113g) of pumice to 8oz (227g) of soap mixture, stir thoroughly and then pour quickly into greased moulds to set. Pumice can be bought in chemists and artists' supply shops.

SEAWEED: The use of seaweed improves the skin's texture and colour and it can be bought in powdered form from health food stores. Although packed with vitamins and minerals, sadly these do not survive the saponification process but seaweed is well worth using for both its therapeutic and decorative qualities.

SPICES: Powdered spices such as cinnamon, paprika and turmeric can be used in soap purely as natural colouring agents (see Colourings on pages 26–27). While cloves have valuable antiseptic qualities they can be irritating and should be avoided when soap is destined for use on sensitive skin.

WHEATGERM: Wheatgerm oil has many beneficial uses in soap (see Precious Additives on pages 15-16) while the germ itself can be powdered and used for its mildly abrasive quality. Add approximately 1 tablespoon (5g) per lb (454g) of soap.

COLOURINGS

the one statement I can make with precision is that soapmaking is an imprecise art. This is particularly evident when it comes to colourings, and much experimentation has taught me that natural is beautiful. Many soapmakers hanker for the lapis blues and brilliant greens that are sometimes evident in mass-produced soaps. These are achieved using natural ultramarines and oxides or specific pigment powders created for cosmetic use.

The major problem with colourings is that the sodium hydroxide (caustic soda/lye) in your soap mix will create a reaction that throws up unexpected results. Blue pigment can produce pink soap (depending on the type of base oils in your soap). This is fine if you want pink soap but very frustrating if you were hoping for blue. The inclusion of honey-coloured beeswax and milk of any kind produces a tan-coloured soap base. If you add blue pigment to this, the result will be a green soap. The most stable colourings come from natural ingredients, such as spices and chocolate, and I list below the shades you can hope to achieve using these additives. Unfortunately, normal food colourings will not work in soap but wax colourings, designed for candlemaking, will.

When using pigments and wax dyes, do not be tempted to make the colour too deep, and always experiment with a test batch first. Your aim is to achieve a bar of soap that retains white bubbles and will not leave a bright pink or blue ring around the bath and colourful splodges on your towels. Bright colours also have a tendency to fade. Divide your test batch and store half in a dark place and the rest in bright light. Check the variation after several weeks to test for colour stability.

natural colourings

Use approximately $\frac{1}{2}$ teaspoon (2.5g) per lb (454g) of soap. Mix with a small amount of soap taken from the batch and

then return to the pot and stir rapidly. Here are the shades that are produced when the following are added to a white base soap mix.

Cayenne pepper – salmon
Cinnamon powder – beige
Cocoa powder – coffee to brown colour
Curry powder – yellow-peach
Paprika – peach
Turmeric – golden yellow
Dark squares of cooking chocolate – brown
Liquid chlorophyll – light green

oxides and cosmetic pigments

These will colour soap but only use minute quantities. When using an ultramarine or an oxide in a 2-lb (900-g) batch of soap, dissolve approximately $\frac{1}{4}$ tsp (4g) of dry powder in 1oz (28g) of warm, distilled water. Remember to reduce the water content of your soap recipe by 1oz (28g) to counteract this. Add the diluted colourant to the soap

mix with a dropper so you can control the colour density. Bear in mind that your soap will look considerably darker in the pot than after it has set. Less powder is required when using cosmetic pigments – dissolve only the tip of a teaspoon (1g) of pigment in 1oz (28g) of water, then proceed as above.

Colourings are best added at trace after the addition of essential oils because these can also affect the basic colour of your soap. Take great care not to ingest pigments because they have varying levels of toxicity. Experiment with the ultramarines, which are available in various colours, and also the ochres and iron oxides.

Lori Schenkelberg, a very enterprising woman in the US, now packages tiny quantities of oxides and cosmetic pigments and also offers soap samples that show you the actual colours you can achieve. She sells her pigment packs by mail order, together with a very useful information sheet (see Stockists on page 79). Lori uses the following basic soap recipe to achieve pure colours:

20oz (567g) vegetable fat (Crisco)
6oz (170g) coconut oil
6oz (170g) palm oil
12oz (340g) distilled water
4½oz (120g) sodium hydroxide (caustic soda/lye)

wax chips

These are designed for candlemaking and can be used with some success to colour soap. Colours can be mixed and matched to create your own shades. Dissolve slivers from the chips in some of the soap mix taken from the pot, then return it to the batch, stirring until evenly mixed.

wax crayons

These can also be used successfully in soapmaking. Treat them in the same manner as wax chips.

soap colouring

Various UK craft manufacturers sell liquid as 'soap colouring'. This is very successful for use with rebatched glycerine soap, for which it was designed, but unfortunately it seldom survives the sodium hydroxide during the saponification process.

recip

If you are a keen cook you will love the combinations of herbs,
spices and vitamin-packed oils that the soaps in this book contain.
Use these recipes only as a guideline. Add your choice of essential
oils and herbal delicacies to create your own very personal soap,
and to design soaps for your friends and family.

On the following pages you will find recipes for soaps for all
occasions. Some are designed for specific purposes, such as kitchen
soap and gardener's soap, while others are created for their scent,
texture and colour. Hopefully, there is something here for everyone.

When I first began to make soaps, my friends were very nervous
about trying them. The assumption seemed to be that if the bar
wasn't neatly shaped and highly polished the soap couldn't be safe
to use. Nowadays, they can't get enough of them. You will soon find
yourself making soap for your friends, your friend's friends and your
friend's children's friends … That's when you start charging.

Please, do try the shampoo bar on page 72. It leaves your hair
feeling clean for much longer than proprietary brands because it
doesn't contain a wax base or harsh chemicals. Olive oil, in
particular, will keep your hair feeling smooth and glossy.

Take great care to measure your ingredients accurately and all will
be well. Make just one batch and you will be well on the way to
becoming a soapaholic.

es

basic soap making

The quality of your soap will improve according to the additives that you select, and the purpose of this book is to encourage you to tailor-make your own soaps to suit your skin type and your fragrance preferences. It is, however, perfectly possible to make soap using one single fat that you probably already have in your refrigerator. The following is a basic step-by-step method that applies to all soap making recipes.

1 Weigh out the base fats, oils and beeswax (if required), using either ounces or grams, but not both.

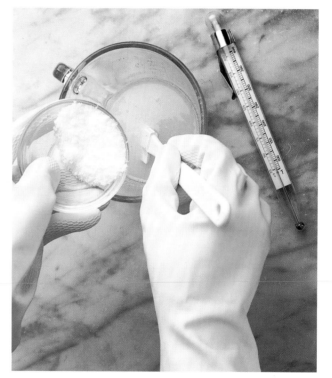

2 Place these ingredients in a stainless steel or enamel pan over a low heat until melted. Turn off the heat and leave until the oils reach approximately 130°F (54.4°C), stirring intermittently.

3 Weigh out the sodium hydroxide (caustic soda/lye) and water.

4 Pour the sodium hydroxide granules into the water and stir until dissolved. Leave until the temperature settles at about 130°F (54°C). Wear eye protection and rubber gloves. Take care not to inhale the fumes.

5 Add the sodium hydroxide solution to the fats and stir carefully.

6 Stir intermittently until the mixture thickens to the point where you can trickle some soap off the back of a spoon and it will leave a trace line on the surface of the mixture. This is called 'trace'.

7 Add the colouring and essential oils as required.

8 Stir and then pour the mixture into the greased mould.

9 Cover the soap with a towel or blanket and leave to set for 24 hours or until hard. Wearing a pair of rubber gloves, turn the soap out of the mould and cut into bars. Cover the soap with a blanket to insulate it and leave to cure for four weeks before use.

The following basic recipes will produce white soaps and are very simple to make. They offer you the chance to experiment with soapmaking without investing in expensive ingredients. To enable you to do this, the following recipes are sized as 1lb (454g) batches.

tally ho!

Made entirely from dripping (tallow), this is a nice, hard soap that is quick to trace.

16oz (454g) dripping (tallow)
2oz (57g) sodium hydroxide (caustic soda/lye)
5oz (142g) distilled or spring water

lardy cake

Many soapmakers have a preference for using lard because it produces a very white soap with large, creamy bubbles. It can have a fatty smell so it is a good idea to disguise this with essential oils.

16oz (454g) lard
2oz (57g) sodium hydroxide (caustic soda/lye)
5oz (142g) distilled or spring water

vegetarian soap

This recipe produces quite a soft soap and will take longer than the other two recipes to trace. Nevertheless, it is a good standby for a rainy day.

16oz (454g) vegetable fat (shortening)
2oz (57g) sodium hydroxide (caustic soda/lye)
5oz (142g) distilled or spring water

Grease a square or oblong mould. Follow the basic method just described. It will take about 30 minutes to reach 'trace'. Add 1 tbsp (15g) of your favourite essential oils if you wish to use them and stir well. Pour the mixture immediately into the mould and cover with a towel or blanket. Leave to set for 24 hours or until the soap reaches a solid consistency. Wearing rubber gloves, remove the soap from the mould. Cut the soap into bars at this stage, then cover the soap and leave to cure for four weeks before use.

fruit soaps

Invariably, soaps that are good for your skin also look and smell good enough to eat. Fruit soaps are no exception and fruit effects can be incorporated into your soaps in a number of ways. While some artificial floral fragrances can be somewhat nondescript, there are some wonderful fruity fragrances on the market. You can also liquidize fresh fruits and incorporate them with your sodium hydroxide/water mix or add citrus zest and/or finely-grated citrus peel to give colour, texture and goodness all at once. Sadly, liquidized blackberries will not result in dark blue soap. Fruits tend to turn brown or grey under the influence of the sodium hydroxide, so extra colouring is needed. Apricot kernel oil is a very precious ingredient which has magical skin-softening powers. Essential oils extracted from citrus fruits do not tend to hold their scent very well so, when using these, it is advisable to add a little benzoin as a fixative.

blackberry smoothy

This soap has the appearance of soft blue suede and I was tempted to add more and more ultramarine powder to achieve a lapis lookalike. Avoid the temptation of adding too much colourant to your soaps as the result is invariably blue-stained towels and a blue ring around the bath. Remember also that your soap mix looks considerably darker than the final colour you will achieve.

soap style:
❑ medium/hard soap with medium bubbles
❑ looks and smells delicious
❑ not recommended for sensitive skins

20oz (567g) vegetable fat (shortening)
6oz (170g) coconut oil
6oz (170g) palm oil
12oz (340g) distilled or spring water
4oz (113g) sodium hydroxide (caustic soda/lye)
½ tsp (2.5g) ultramarine powder
2 tsp (10g) blackberry fragrance oil

Grease a square or oblong mould. Place the fat and base oils in a stainless steel or enamel pot over a low heat. Set aside ½oz (14g) of water and pour the remainder into a heavy glass or plastic bowl or jug. Wearing rubber gloves and eye protection, add the sodium hydroxide (caustic soda/lye) to the water and stir until dissolved. When the oils have melted, remove them from the heat.

Place one sugar thermometer in the oils and one in the caustic solution. When both thermometers reach an equal temperature between 120°F (49°C) and 140°F (60°C), pour the caustic solution into the oil. (See pages 31-32 for more information.) Stir occasionally until the mixture reaches trace. This should take about 90 minutes.

Take the water you have set aside and add to it the ultramarine powder. Stir until this has completely dissolved and then add the mixture gradually to the soap. Add the blackberry fragrance and stir well. Pour immediately into the mould and cover with a towel or blanket. Leave to set for 24 hours or until the soap reaches a solid consistency. Wearing rubber gloves, remove the soap from the mould and cut into blocks. Cover the soap and leave to cure for four weeks before use.

peach melba

This creamy summer soap has a heady peach and geranium fragrance and the silky-soft qualities of glycerine and apricot kernel oil. The colouring is mottled more by accident than design, but then among the pleasures of soapmaking are

grapefruit slice (top), peach melba (centre), blackberry smoothy (bottom)

the surprises you create along the way. I have used plastic microwave dishes for my moulds but you can, of course, choose any shape you wish.

soap style:
- ❏ extra-smooth and creamy
- ❏ omit the colouring for a wonderful face soap
- ❏ medium bubbles

12oz (340g) vegetable oil

10oz (283g) coconut oil

9oz (255g) olive oil

13oz (368g) distilled or spring water

4½ oz (127g) sodium hydroxide (caustic soda/lye)

1 tsp (5g) finely-grated red candle wax colouring

1 tbsp (15g) glycerine

1 tbsp (15g) apricot kernel oil

1 tsp (5g) geranium essential oil

1 tsp (5g) peach fragrance oil

Grease your chosen moulds. Place the base oils in a stainless steel or enamel pot over a low heat. Pour the water into a heavy glass or plastic bowl or jug. Wearing rubber gloves and eye protection, add the sodium hydroxide (caustic soda/lye) to the water and stir until dissolved. When the oils have melted, remove them from the heat.

Place one sugar thermometer in the oils and one in the caustic solution. When both thermometers reach an equal temperature between 120°F (49°C) and 140°F (60°C), pour the caustic solution into the oil. (See pages 31-32 for more information.) Stir occasionally until the mixture reaches trace. This should take about 90 minutes.

Take 1 tbsp (15g) of soap from the pot and place it in a cup with the wax colouring flakes. Mix until they have dissolved, then return the mixture to the pot and stir thoroughly. Add the glycerine, apricot, essential and fragrance oils, and stir well. Pour immediately into the moulds and cover with a towel or blanket. Leave to set for 24 hours or until the soap reaches a solid consistency.

a *pricots and peaches are popular and well-loved fruits, yet they are in fact part of the rose family. This no doubt contributes to their rich perfume.*

Wearing rubber gloves, remove the soap from the moulds and cut if required. Cover the soap and leave to cure for four weeks before use.

grapefruit slice

This is a soap to wake you up on the morning after. Tangy and fresh and made in a PVC pipe, you can create whole grapefruit slices or cut them into semicircles as I have done. For extra zing and texture, add 1 tbsp (15g) of finely-grated grapefruit peel at trace.

soap style:
- ❏ good for greasy skin
- ❏ medium/hard soap with medium bubbles

24oz (680g) vegetable fat (shortening)

8oz (227g) coconut oil

2oz (57g) beeswax

11oz (312g) distilled or spring water

5oz (142g) sodium hydroxide (caustic soda/lye)

½ tsp (2.5g) verdant blue liquid soap colouring (see Stockists on page 80)

1 tbsp (15g) grapefruit essential oil

½ tsp (2.5g) powdered or tincture of benzoin

Grease the inside of a 4-in (10-cm) diameter length of PVC pipe that is at least 10in (25cm) long. Place the fat, oil and beeswax in a stainless steel or enamel pot over a low heat. Pour the water into a heavy glass or plastic bowl or jug. Wearing rubber gloves and eye protection, add the sodium hydroxide (caustic soda/lye) to the water and stir until dissolved. When the oils have melted, remove them from the heat.

Place one sugar thermometer in the oils and one in the caustic solution. When both thermometers reach an equal temperature between 120°F (49°C) and 140°F (60°C), pour the caustic solution into the fats. (See pages 30-31 for more information.) Stir occasionally until the mixture reaches trace. This should take about 15 minutes.

Add the colouring, essential oil and benzoin and stir well. Pour immediately into the mould and cover with a towel or blanket. Leave to set for 24 hours or until the soap reaches a solid consistency. Wearing rubber gloves, remove the soap from the mould and cut into slices. Cover the soap and leave to cure for four weeks before use.

strawberry soap

I went to town with this soap, adding red pigment and strawberry fragrance together with a whole punnet of fresh berries. In theory, the fresh strawberries should introduce an astringent quality but I fear any therapeutic value is probably diminished by the addition of the artificial colourant and fragrance oil. This is a nice soap to include in a mixed basket as it will certainly add colour, texture and interest.

soap style:
- ❏ medium/soft soap with medium bubbles
- ❏ great accessory for a brightly coloured bathroom
- ❏ not recommended for sensitive skins

12oz (340g) vegetable fat (shortening)

8oz (227g) tallow (dripping)

8oz (227g) coconut oil

4oz (113g) olive oil

2oz (57g) beeswax

14oz (397g) distilled or spring water

6oz (170g) fresh strawberries

5oz (142g) sodium hydroxide (caustic soda/lye)

½ tsp (2.5g) diluted red cosmetic pigment (D&C red 28)

1oz (28g) wheatgerm oil

2 tsp (10g) strawberry fragrance oil

Grease your chosen mould. Place the fats, base oils and beeswax in a stainless steel or enamel pot over a low heat. Set aside 4oz (113g) of the water and pour the remainder into a heavy glass or plastic bowl or jug.

Remove the leaves and stalks from the fresh strawberries and place them in a liquidizer, adding the water you set aside. Run the machine until the strawberries are reduced to liquid, then add this to the rest of the water. Wearing rubber gloves and eye protection, add the sodium hydroxide (caustic soda/lye) to the strawberry liquid and stir until dissolved. When the oils have melted, remove them from the heat.

Place one sugar thermometer in the oils and one in the caustic solution. When both thermometers reach an equal temperature between 120°F (49°C) and 140°F (60°C), pour the caustic solution into the oil. (See pages 31-32 for more information.) Stir occasionally until the mixture reaches trace. This should take about 30 minutes.

Add the colouring, then add the wheatgerm and fragrance oil and stir well. Pour immediately into the mould and cover with a towel or blanket. Leave to set for 48 hours or until the soap reaches a solid consistency. Wearing rubber gloves, remove the soap from the mould and cut into blocks. Cover the soap and leave to cure for four weeks before use.

fresh as a cucumber

This interesting little soap contains fresh cucumber which produces bright green flecks. To preserve these I have included a few drops of Grapefruit Seed Extract which also speeds up the trace time. Unable to find a cucumber fragrance oil, I perfumed this soap with pear.

soap style:
- ❏ medium hard with creamy bubbles
- ❏ decorative soap
- ❏ good for all skin types

14 oz (395g) coconut oil
10 oz (282g) vegetable fat (shortening)
8 oz (226g) olive oil
1 cup of fresh cucumber (unpeeled and cut into chunks)
$14\frac{1}{2}$ oz (415g) distilled or spring water
$5\frac{1}{2}$ oz (143g) sodium hydroxide (lye)
$\frac{1}{2}$ tsp (2.5 ml) GSE (Grapefruit Seed Extract)
1 tbs (15 ml) pear fragrance oil

Grease the mould. Weigh out the fats, base oils and place them over a low heat. While the fats are melting, weigh the water and pour it into a heavy glass or plastic bowl or jug. Add the cucumber chunks and liquidise to a pulp. Wearing rubber gloves and eye protection, add the sodium hydroxide (lye) to the water/cucumber and stir until dissolved. When the oils and fats have melted, remove them from the heat. Place one sugar thermometer in the oils and one in the caustic solution. When both thermometers reach an equal temperature between 120°F (49°C) and 140°F (60°C), pour the caustic solution into the oil. Stir intermittently until the mixture thickens to the point of 'trace'. This should take around 20 minutes.

Add the pear fragrance and stir well. Pour immediately into the mould and cover with a towel or blanket. Leave to set for 24 hours or until the soap reaches a solid consistency. Wearing rubber gloves, push the soap out of the pipe and cut into slices. Cover the soap and leave to cure for four weeks before use.

st clements

This soap contains the finely grated rind of oranges and lemons with a touch of benzoin to preserve them. I used turmeric as a colourant but you could replace this with a cosmetic pigment.

soap style:
- ❏ hard and waxy with medium bubbles
- ❏ long lasting
- ❏ good for greasy skin

14 oz (395g) vegetable oil
10 oz (282g) coconut oil
8 oz (226g) palm oil
2 oz (56.5g) beeswax
$10\frac{1}{2}$ oz (297g) distilled or spring water
$5\frac{1}{2}$ oz (143g) sodium hydroxide (lye)
4 oz (113g) orange flower water
1 cup mixed, finely grated fresh orange and lemon rind
2 tsps powdered turmeric
1 tbs (15 ml) each of orange and lemon essential oils
1 tsp liquid or powdered benzoin

Make in the usual way (see pages 31-32). Trace should take 10 minutes.

Just before trace, sprinkle in the citrus peel and stir thoroughly. At trace add the essential oils, benzoin and turmeric and stir well. Pour immediately into the mould and cover with a towel and blanket. Leave to set for 24 hours or until the soap reaches a solid consistency. Wearing rubber gloves, turn the soap out of the mould and cut into chunks. Cover the soap and leave to cure for four weeks before use.

floral soaps

Jasmine and rose petals are among the most precious of all floral essences, while essential oils from lavender buds have useful antiseptic and anti-depressant properties. Calendula (pot marigold) is another valuable resource for the soapmaker and particularly soothing for chapped and split skin. While rarely available as a pure essential oil, calendula petals can be infused in olive oil or added to a soap mixture in dried petal form.

You can replace the water content in the following recipes with shop-bought rosewater or homemade floral waters (see pages 20-21). If you want the luxury of essential oils, mix and match floral oils to create your own personal bouquet.

pink lavender & lime soap

The delicate, pale pink colour of this soap was actually created with a blue pigment. If you want a lavender blue colour, follow this recipe but leave out the essential oils and the pigment. Leave the soap for at least two weeks, then grate it down and rebatch it, following the instructions on page 18.

soap style:
- ❏ good antiseptic qualities
- ❏ great for greasy skin
- ❏ hard soap with large bubbles

8oz (227g) beef dripping (tallow)
8oz (227g) coconut oil
16oz (454g) vegetable fat (shortening)
4¾oz (134g) sodium hydroxide (caustic soda/lye)
13¾oz (389g) distilled or spring water
2 tsp (10g) blue liquid soap colouring
2 tsp (10g) lavender essential oil
1 tsp (5g) lime essential oil
1 tsp (5g) liquid benzoin

Grease a shallow square or oblong mould.

Weigh out the fats and base oils and place them over a low heat in a stainless steel or enamel pot.

While the fats are melting, weigh the water and pour this into a heavy glass or plastic bowl or jug.

Wearing rubber gloves and eye protection, add the sodium hydroxide (lye) to the water and stir until dissolved. When the oils and fats have melted, remove them from the heat. Place one sugar thermometer in the oils and one in the caustic solution. When both thermometers reach an equal temperature between 120°F (49°C) and 140°F (60°C), pour the caustic solution into the oil. (See pages 31-32 for more information.) Stir intermittently until the mixture thickens to the point where you can trickle some soap off the back of a spoon and it will leave a trace line on the top of the mixture. This should take about 40 minutes.

r *ose oils used to be applied to the eyelids to create a sheen and, in times before dental care existed, pastilles made from myrrh and rose petals crushed in honey were chewed to sweeten the breath. One of the most famous perfumes made from the rose was Red Rose, produced by Floris of London during the reign of King Edward VII.*

Add the colouring and the essential oils and stir well. Pour immediately into the mould and cover with a towel or blanket. Leave to set for 24 hours or until the soap reaches a solid consistency.

Wearing rubber gloves, remove the soap from the mould. If you have used a slab mould cut the soap into bars at this stage. Cover the soap and leave to cure for four weeks before use.

buttered roses with a hint of spice

The price of a pure oil of rose could leave you blowing bubbles, but fortunately you can buy inexpensive man-made rose fragrance oils that, for the purposes of soapmaking, are a good substitute. Combined with sunflower oil, cocoa butter and a hint of cardamom, that hot soak at the end of a long, hard day could prove a truly exotic experience.

soap style:
- ❑ relieves stress and tension
- ❑ hard but creamy soap with large bubbles

10oz (283g) coconut oil
10oz (283g) vegetable fat (shortening)
8oz (227g) sunflower oil
4oz (113g) cocoa butter
4¾oz (134g) sodium hydroxide (caustic soda/lye)
13¾oz (389g) distilled or spring water
2 tsp (10g) red liquid soap colouring
2 tsp (10g) English rose fragrance oil
1 tsp (5g) cardamom essential oil
½ tsp (2.5g) liquid benzoin

Make this soap in the same way as the Pink Lavender and Lime Soap, above. However, you should reach the trace stage in about 15 minutes.

sunflower & calendula

Sunflower oil contains valuable vitamins and minerals. Add the soothing properties of calendula and you have a soap for all seasons and one that would make a lovely gift.

soap style:
- ❑ good for all skin types
- ❑ a medium/hard bar with a frothy lather and creamy texture

12oz (340g) coconut oil
12oz (340g) sunflower oil
8oz (227g) palm oil
5¼oz (149g) sodium
   hydroxide (lye)
14¼oz (404g) distilled
   or spring water
1 tsp (5g) turmeric
3 tbsp (45g) dried
   calendula petals
2 tsp (10g) clary sage oil
2 tsp (10g) marjoram oil

Grease your mould with vegetable fat. Make the soap in the same manner as the Pink Lavender and Lime Soap above, but when you begin to measure the temperature of the two mixtures, wait until both thermometers reach an equal temperature between 130°F (54°C) and 150°F (65°C). Pour the caustic solution into the fats and stir. Stir intermittently until the mixture reaches trace. As a guide this should take around 40 minutes.

Add the turmeric and essential oils and stir well. Now add the dried flower petals and stir vigorously. Pour immediately into the mould and cover with a towel or blanket. Leave to set for 12 hours or until the soap reaches a near solid consistency.

Wearing rubber gloves, remove the soap from the mould. If you have used a slab mould, cut the soap into bars at this stage. Cover the soap and leave to cure for five weeks before use.

the marigold can be used as a talisman, but to be truly lucky it must be picked when the sun enters the sign of Virgo and wrapped together with a wolf's tooth in a bay leaf. If you dream of calendula in full bloom you can be certain of coming wealth. For the less mystic-minded, try rubbing the flower head on a bee or wasp sting; tradition says that this brings instant relief.

honey & beeswax soaps

Soaps that contain beeswax have numerous advantages: they trace quickly; result in a pleasing, hard texture; and the smell of honey in the beeswax is simply glorious. I tend to use honey-coloured, purified beeswax which I buy from a local bee-keeper. You can also buy it in 1oz (28g) ingots from good furniture shops who use it to beautify wood. The beeswax generally used in cosmetic lotions and potions is white and can be bought in pellets or straps from specialist aromatherapy suppliers. Honey is, by itself, a wonderful emollient and is packed with vitamins but it will soften the soap if you use too much and can sometimes cause separation. The following recipes are among my favourites and very popular with my friends.

cinnamon, honey & almond soap cakes

These really are good enough to eat, especially when topped with slivers of almond and cut into blocks with a biscuit-cutter. You could also use individual hexagonal moulds to give the impression of a honeycomb. The almonds will help to unplug the pores and exfoliate the skin yet, provided they are finely ground, will not result in a coarse, scrubby bar.

soap style:
- ❏ medium/soft with small, creamy bubbles
- ❏ aromatic

18oz (510g) vegetable fat (shortening)
6oz (170g) olive oil
6oz (170g) coconut oil
1½oz (42g) beeswax
14oz (397g) distilled or spring water
5oz (142g) sodium hydroxide (caustic soda/lye)
1 tbsp (15g) finely ground almonds
1 tbsp (15g) ground cinnamon
2oz (57g) sweet almond oil
2 tsp (10g) each of ylang-ylang and nutmeg essential oils
1 tsp (5g) benzoin
1 tbsp (15g) honey
1 tbsp (15g) flaked almonds (for decoration only)

Grease a shallow square or oblong mould. Place the fat, base oils and beeswax in a stainless steel or enamel pot over a low heat. Pour the water into a heavy glass or plastic bowl or jug. Wearing rubber gloves and eye protection, add the sodium hydroxide (caustic soda/lye) to the water and stir until dissolved. When the oils have melted, remove them from the heat.

Place one sugar thermometer in the oils and one in the caustic solution. When both thermometers reach an equal temperature between 120°F (49°C) and 140°F (60°C), pour the caustic solution into the oil. (See pages 31-32 for more information.) Stir occasionally until the mixture reaches trace. This should take about 20 minutes.

Sprinkle the ground almonds and cinnamon into the mix and stir well. Add the sweet almond and essential oils together with the benzoin and honey. Stir well. Pour immediately into the mould and cover with a towel or blanket. Leave to set for 24 hours or until the soap reaches a solid consistency. Wearing rubber gloves, press the almond flakes into the surface of the soap and cut into shapes with a biscuit-cutter if required. Cover the soap and leave to cure for four weeks before use.

beeswax, honey & oatmeal scrub

This is a lovely, crunchy soap that leaves you feeling clean and shiny. I have used it for complete bars and also as a layer on top of a smooth soap so that you can choose when you wish to use the scrubby bit. Adjust the amount of oatmeal according to how rough you want the finished bar to be. I chose to add orange essential oil and you could complement this by substituting some of the oats with finely-ground dried orange peel.

soap style:
❑ scrubby bar with large bubbles
❑ good for all skin types

10oz (283g) vegetable fat (shortening)
12oz (340g) olive oil
10oz (283g) coconut oil
2oz (57g) beeswax
11oz (312g) distilled or spring water
5oz (142g) sodium hydroxide (caustic soda/lye)

2oz (57g) medium oatmeal (not instant porridge oats)
2 tbsp (30g) honey
1 tbsp (15g) each of orange and clary sage essential oils

Grease a shallow square or oblong mould. Place the fat, base oils and beeswax in a stainless steel or enamel pot over a low heat. Pour the water into a heavy glass or plastic bowl or jug. Wearing rubber gloves and eye protection, add the sodium hydroxide (caustic soda/lye) to the water and stir until dissolved. When the oils have melted, remove them from the heat.

Place one sugar thermometer in the oils and one in the caustic solution. When both thermometers reach an equal temperature between 120°F (49°C) and 140°F (60°C), pour the caustic solution into the oil. Stir occasionally until the mixture reaches trace. This should take about 35 minutes.

Sprinkle the oatmeal into the mix and stir well. Add the honey and the essential oils. Stir well. Pour immediately into the mould and cover with a towel or blanket. Leave to set for 24 hours or until the soap reaches a solid consistency. Wearing rubber gloves, turn the soap out of the mould and cut into chunks. Cover the soap and leave to cure for four weeks before use.

honey blossom

This is a lovely, gentle soap with no artificial colouring. Any scent is a product of the beeswax and honey. I have used this in a layered batch with the Beeswax, Honey and Oatmeal Scrub on the top, and that really gives you the best of both worlds. Try infusing the almond oil with your favourite blossoms before making the soap – see pages 20-23 for instructions on how to do this.

soap style:
❑ hard soap with large bubbles
❑ creamy texture
❑ good for all skin types

15oz (425g) vegetable fat (shortening)
10oz (283g) sweet almond oil
7oz (198g) olive oil
2oz (57g) white beeswax
10oz (283g) distilled or spring water
5oz (142g) sodium hydroxide (caustic soda/lye)
2 tbsp (30g) honey

Grease a shallow square or oblong mould. Place the fat, base oils and beeswax in a stainless steel or enamel pot over a low heat. Pour the water into a heavy glass or plastic bowl or jug. Wearing rubber gloves and eye protection, add the sodium hydroxide (caustic soda/lye) to the water and stir until dissolved. When the oils have melted, remove them from the heat.

Place one sugar thermometer in the oils and one in the caustic solution. When both thermometers reach an equal temperature between 120°F (49°C) and 140°F (60°C), pour the caustic solution into the oil. (See pages 31-32 for more information.) Stir occasionally until the mixture reaches trace. This should take about 20 minutes.

Add the honey and stir well. Pour immediately into the mould and cover with a towel or blanket. Leave to set for 24 hours or until the soap reaches a solid consistency. Wearing rubber gloves, remove the soap from the mould and cut into bars. Cover the soap and leave to cure for four weeks before use.

To make an Oatmeal/Honey Blossom Layered Soap, pour the Honey Blossom mixture into the mould, filling it to the halfway point. Set aside for at least a week without removing it from the mould. Make the Beeswax, Honey and Oatmeal Scrub as described above and pour this over the Honey Blossom, filling the mould to the brim. Leave to set for 48 hours then turn out of the mould, cut into bars and trim. Cover the soap and leave to cure for four weeks before use.

herb & spice soaps

Herbs can create interesting textures in your soaps and also provide that natural, country look reminiscent of all things wholesome. They can be added to your soap in the form of essential oils, or as dried herbs scattered into the mixture at trace. You can also use herb-infused oils as a base for your soap – instructions for infusing oils are given on pages 20-23. Pulverized fresh herbs can be included with the water content although they may lose their fresh, clean, green appearance quite quickly. Powdered spices are natural colourants (see Colourings on pages 26-27) and combinations of their essential oils can create clear, warming fragrances.

pink marble

This soap has a wonderful, smooth, shiny texture and its mottled colouring closely resembles marble. I have gone to town on the spices, using lots of ginger and cardamom oil with just a touch of red oxide for the colouring.

soap style:
- ❑ hard and long-lasting with large bubbles and quick lather
- ❑ warming fragrance
- ❑ not recommended for sensitive skins

12oz (340g) dripping (tallow)
8oz (227g) palm oil
8oz (227g) coconut oil
4oz (113g) olive oil
14oz (397g) distilled or spring water
5oz (142g) sodium hydroxide (caustic soda/lye)
1 tsp (5g) diluted red oxide (see pages 26-27)
2 tsp (10g) ginger essential oil
1 tsp (5g) cardamom essential oil

Grease a shallow square or oblong mould. Place the fat and base oils in a stainless steel or enamel pot over a low heat. Pour the water into a heavy glass or plastic bowl or jug. Wearing rubber gloves and eye protection, add the sodium hydroxide (caustic soda/lye) to the water and stir until dissolved. When the oils have melted, remove them from the heat.

Place one sugar thermometer in the oils and one in the caustic solution. When both thermometers reach an equal temperature between 120°F (49°C) and 140°F (60°C), pour the caustic solution into the oil. (See pages 31-32 for more information.) Stir occasionally until the mixture reaches trace. This should take about 20 minutes.

Add the colouring and essential oils and stir well. Pour immediately into the mould and cover with a towel or blanket. Leave to set for 24 hours or until the soap reaches a solid consistency. Wearing rubber gloves, remove the soap from the mould and cut into bars. Cover the soap and leave to cure for four weeks before use.

oatmeal & lemon balm scrub bar

This is a good wake-you-up bar with a scrubby texture and a fresh perfume. I have used oatmeal to create the texture but you could include a handful of dried lemon balm for added effect.

soap style:
- ❏ medium/soft with a rough texture
- ❏ medium bubbles

24oz (680g) vegetable fat (shortening)
8oz (227g) coconut oil
2oz (57g) beeswax
11oz (312g) distilled or spring water
5oz (142g) sodium hydroxide (caustic soda/lye)
3oz (85g) oatmeal or mixture of oatmeal and dried
    lemon balm
1 tsp (5g) diluted ultramarine powder (see Colourings on
    pages 26-27)
1 tbsp (15g) clary sage essential oil
2 tsp (10g) lemon essential oil

Grease a shallow square or oblong mould. Place the fat, oil and beeswax in a stainless steel or enamel pot over a low heat. Pour the water into a heavy glass or plastic bowl or jug. Wearing rubber gloves and eye protection, add the sodium hydroxide (caustic soda/lye) to the water and stir until dissolved. When the oils have melted, remove them from the heat. Place one sugar thermometer in the oils and one in the caustic solution. When both thermometers reach

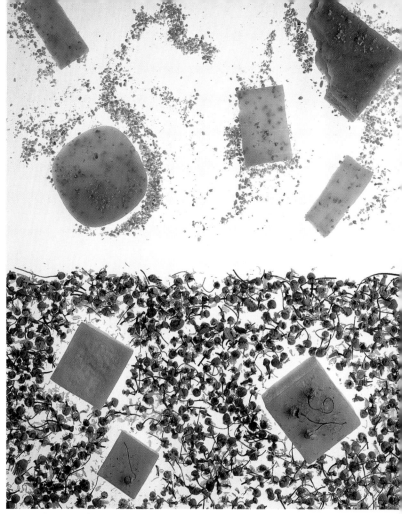

camomile tea bar (bottom), oatmeal and lemon balm scrub bar (top)

an equal temperature between 120°F (49°C) and 140°F (60°C), pour the caustic solution into the oil. Stir occasionally until the mixture reaches trace. This should take about 30 minutes.

Add the oatmeal or mixture of oatmeal and lemon balm, ultramarine and essential oils and stir well. Pour immediately into the mould and cover with a towel or blanket. Leave to set for 24 hours or until the soap reaches a solid consistency. Wearing rubber gloves, remove the soap from the mould and cut into bars. Cover the soap and leave it to cure for four weeks before use.

camomile tea bar

The shops are full of a wonderful variety of fruit and herbal teas and these can be used to great effect in your soap. This camomile bar also works well as a shampoo and is particularly effective on blonde hair.

natural wonder bar

soap style:
- ❏ medium soap with large bubbles
- ❏ creamy lather
- ❏ good for all skin types

15oz (425g) distilled or spring water

2 camomile teabags

18oz (510g) coconut oil

8oz (227g) olive oil

6oz (170g) sweet almond oil

5½oz (156g) sodium hydroxide (caustic soda/lye)

2 tsp (10g) camomile essential oil

1 tsp (5g) lemon grass essential oil

Grease a shallow square or oblong mould. Boil the water and pour it into a glass or enamel jug. Drop in the teabags and cover with a lid. Leave to cool.

Place the base oils in a stainless steel or enamel pot over a low heat. Remove the teabags from the water and, wearing rubber gloves and eye protection, add the sodium hydroxide (caustic soda/lye) to the cold tea and stir until dissolved. When the oils have melted, remove them from the heat.

Place one sugar thermometer in the oils and one in the caustic solution. When both thermometers reach an equal temperature between 120°F (49°C) and 140°F (60°C), pour the caustic solution into the oil. (See pages 31-32 for more information.) Stir occasionally until the mixture reaches trace. This could take up to 2 hours.

Open the used teabags and scatter the tea leaves into the mixture. Add the essential oils and stir thoroughly. Pour immediately into the mould and cover with a towel or blanket. Leave to set for 48 hours or until the soap reaches a solid consistency. Wearing rubber gloves, remove the soap from the mould and cut into bars. Cover the soap and leave to cure for four weeks before use.

tip

While dock leaves are a well-known remedy for nettle stings, the juice of the nettle itself will also soothe the sting. Stinging nettles are an excellent substitute for spinach and are widely used to create chlorophyll. Liquid chlorophyll is a natural green colouring for your soap.

natural wonder bar

Because the sting from a nettle can be nasty, the therapeutic value of this common weed is often overlooked. Nettles have stimulating and astringent qualities and a nettle infusion is beneficial when applied to cuts, burns and scalds. This soap can also be used as a shampoo bar which is rumoured to reduce balding.

soap style:
- ❏ soft bar with creamy lather
- ❏ astringent and antiseptic qualities
- ❏ useful as a shampoo

22oz (623g) olive oil

4oz (113g) sweet almond oil

4oz (113g) castor oil

1oz (28g) apricot oil

2oz (57g) white beeswax

10oz (283g) distilled or spring water

2 cups full of young stinging nettle leaves (picked with gloves on!)

4oz (113g) sodium hydroxide (caustic soda/lye)

½oz (14g) wheatgerm oil

2 tsp (10g) tea tree essential oil

1 tsp (5g) rosemary essential oil

Grease a shallow square or oblong mould. Place the four oils, and the beeswax, in a stainless steel or enamel pot over a low heat. Add the water to the nettles. Run this through the liquidizer and pour into a heavy glass or plastic bowl or jug. Wearing rubber gloves and eye protection, add the sodium hydroxide to the liquidized nettles and stir until dissolved. When the oils have melted, remove them from the heat.

Place one sugar thermometer in the oils and one in the caustic solution. When both thermometers reach an equal temperature between 120°F (49°C) and 140°F (60°C), pour the caustic solution into the oil. (See pages 31-32 for more information.) Stir occasionally until the mixture reaches trace. This should take about 50 minutes.

Add the wheatgerm and essential oils and stir well. Pour immediately into the mould and cover with a towel or blanket. Leave to set for 48 hours or until the soap reaches a solid consistency. Wearing rubber gloves, remove the soap from the mould and cut into bars. Cover the soap and leave to cure for four weeks before use.

dairy soaps

There is something gloriously decadent about bathing in milk and, when used as a soapmaking ingredient, milk supplies exactly the creamy rich texture one would expect. I have had great success with the use of goats' milk, although I know many soapers who have experienced various problems. Firstly, goats' milk will turn your soap a deep honey (even orange) colour, so avoid using it if you intend to add pigments. Secondly, it has a tendency to curdle. To avoid this, warm the milk to just above room temperature and add it to the water before mixing with sodium hydroxide (caustic soda/lye). If you find the milk still causes your soap to curdle, mix the soap thoroughly with an electric mixer until it becomes smooth, then pour the soapmix into moulds in the normal way. Dried milk can be used as a substitute for fresh milk but the use of fresh cows' milk can be tricky and result in a mess that smells strongly of ammonia. Eggs, as we all know, are packed with protein and are a valuable addition to both soap and shampoo bars.

poached egg soap

So-named because I used microwave egg poaching dishes as a mould. I perfumed this batch with amber fragrance oil which has a warming, sensual undertone. You could also add a little yellow soap colouring to complete the effect although, without colouring, this recipe produces a mottled creamy-white bar.

soap style:
- ❑ medium/hard soap with large bubbles
- ❑ interesting grainy texture
- ❑ good for all skin types but omit the fragrance if you have sensitive skin

9oz (255g) olive oil

3 egg yolks

12oz (340g) coconut oil

12oz (340g) vegetable fat (shortening)

14½oz (410g) distilled or spring water

5oz (142g) sodium hydroxide (caustic soda/lye)

1 tbsp (15g) vitamin E oil

2 tsp (10g) amber fragrance oil

Grease the inside of your individual or slab mould. Set aside 1oz (28g) of olive oil and whisk this up with the egg yolks. Place the remaining base oils and fat in a stainless steel or enamel pot over a low heat. Pour the water into a heavy glass or plastic bowl or jug. Wearing rubber gloves and eye protection, add the sodium hydroxide (caustic soda/lye) to the water and stir until dissolved. When the oils have melted, remove them from the heat.

Place one sugar thermometer in the oils and one in the caustic solution. When both thermometers reach an equal temperature between 120°F (49°C) and 140°F (60°C), pour the caustic solution into the oil. (See pages 30-31 for more information.) Stir occasionally until the mixture reaches trace. This should take about 35 minutes.

Whisk in the egg/olive oil mixture a little at a time, then add the vitamin E and fragrance oil and stir well. Pour immediately into the moulds and cover with a towel or blanket. Leave to set for 24 hours or until the soap reaches a solid consistency. Wearing rubber gloves, remove the soap from mould and, if necessary, cut into slices. Cover the soap and leave to cure for four weeks before use.

milk chocolate soap bar (top left), goats' milk and ylang-ylang (top right)

milk chocolate soap bar

Chocolate soap is great fun but should be kept away from children or they are bound to end up with a mouthful of bubbles. The amount of chocolate you add will affect both the colour and the fragrance, so I leave the choice to you. Here I have used ½oz (14g) of plain cooking chocolate to create a milky-beige colour.

soap style:
- ❏ hard soap with large bubbles
- ❏ creamy texture

12oz (340g) vegetable fat (shortening)
8oz (227g) tallow (dripping)
12oz (340g) coconut oil
½oz (14g) plain cooking chocolate
10oz (283g) distilled or spring water
4½oz (127g) goats' milk
5oz (142g) sodium hydroxide (caustic soda/lye)

Grease your chosen mould. Place the fats, base oil and chocolate in a stainless steel or enamel pot over a low heat. Pour the water and milk into a heavy glass or plastic bowl or jug. Wearing rubber gloves and eye protection, add the sodium hydroxide (caustic soda/lye) to the liquids and stir until dissolved. When the oils have melted, remove them from the heat.

Place one sugar thermometer in the oils and one in the caustic solution. When both thermometers reach an equal temperature between 120°F (49°C) and 140°F (60°C), pour the caustic solution into the oil. (See pages 31-32 for more information.) Stir occasionally until the mixture reaches trace. This should take about 40 minutes.

Pour immediately into the mould and cover with a towel or blanket. Leave to set for 24 hours or until the soap reaches a solid consistency. Wearing rubber gloves, remove the soap from the mould and cut into slices. Cover the soap and leave to cure for four weeks before use.

goats' milk and ylang-ylang

This is one of my favourite soaps, mainly because of its creamy texture but also because I find ylang-ylang both evocative and refreshing. It is not a soap that produces a particularly good lather but it leaves your skin feeling wonderfully soft and smooth. Try it!

soap style:
- ❏ medium/soft soap with small bubbles
- ❏ creamy texture

8oz (227g) vegetable fat (shortening)
12oz (340g) olive oil
12oz (340g) sunflower oil
2oz (57g) beeswax
10oz (283g) fresh goats' milk
4½oz (127g) sodium hydroxide (caustic soda/lye)
1 tbsp (15g) ylang-ylang essential oil

Grease your chosen mould. Place the fat, base oils and beeswax in a stainless steel or enamel pot over a low heat. Pour the milk into a heavy glass or plastic bowl or jug. Wearing rubber gloves and eye protection, add the sodium hydroxide (caustic soda/lye) to the milk and stir until dissolved. When the oils have melted, remove them from the heat.

Place one sugar thermometer in the oils and one in the caustic solution. When both thermometers reach an equal temperature between 120°F (49°C) and 140°F (60°C), pour the caustic solution into the oil. (See pages 31-32 for more information.) Stir occasionally until the mixture reaches trace. This should take about 90 minutes.

Add the essential oil and stir well. Pour immediately into the mould and cover with a towel or blanket. Leave to set for 24 hours or until the soap reaches a solid consistency. Wearing rubber gloves, remove the soap from the mould and cut into blocks. Cover the soap and leave to cure for four weeks before use.

In Roman times a lady's toilette included a bath in asses' milk, which produced a delicate whiteness to the skin. Her pale face was then freshened and revived with enamel and her rounded eyelids coloured with a needle dipped in jetty dye.

castile soaps

Castile soap, which is probably the finest you can buy or make, is created almost entirely from olive oil. Originating in the Spanish region of Castile (or Castilla, if you happen to be Spanish), the combination of sunshine and an abundant olive harvest might result in the planning of frequent Spanish holidays for everyone who makes and uses the following recipes. Olive oil is available in various grades. Virgin oil is the result of the first pressing and is the purest grade that you can buy. Common or dyer's oil comes from the second pressing and contains a percentage of mucous matter. Pomace or expressed oil is the third pressing and contains a high percentage of mucous and fibrous matter. Olive oil is generally expensive, with the cost varying from year to year depending on the harvest. Fortunately for the soapmaker, the cheapest-quality oil offers the greatest advantages in the saponification process.

salad days soap

This is a nice, white soap with a high percentage of olive oil and the tangy scent of marjoram and fennel. For a mould I stole the flimsy plastic tray used in the supermarket to hold pots of chocolate mousse.

soap style:
- ❑ hard and waxy with large bubbles
- ❑ rich, creamy lather
- ❑ moisturizing

24oz (680g) olive oil
8oz (227g) palm oil
2oz (57g) white beeswax
10oz (283g) distilled or spring water
5oz (142g) sodium hydroxide (caustic soda/lye)
1 tbsp (15g) avocado oil
2 tsp (10g) marjoram essential oil
1 tsp (5g) fennel essential oil

Grease a tray of circular moulds. Place the base oils and beeswax in a stainless steel or enamel pot over a low heat. Pour the water into a heavy glass or plastic bowl or jug. Wearing rubber gloves and eye protection, add the sodium hydroxide to the water and stir until dissolved. When the oils have melted, remove from the heat.

dream castile (top), olive splendour (second one down)

Place one sugar thermometer in the oils and one in the caustic solution. When both thermometers reach an equal temperature between 120°F (49°C) and 140°F (60°C), pour the caustic solution into the oil. Stir occasionally until the mixture reaches trace. This should take about 40 minutes.

Add the avocado and essential oils and stir well. Pour immediately into the moulds and cover with a towel or blanket. Leave to set for 24 hours or until the soap reaches a solid consistency. Wearing rubber gloves, remove the soap from the moulds and trim to shape. Cover the soap and leave to cure for four weeks.

dream castile

Well, here we have it! This is my favourite soap, used consistently as a shampoo and as a rich, creamy, facial soap. Horribly expensive to make but absolutely worth every penny. I keep these bars under lock and key because it physically hurts me to part with one.

soap style:
- ❏ hard soap with large, creamy bubbles
- ❏ moisturizing
- ❏ excellent shampoo bar

30oz (849g) olive oil
2oz (57g) beeswax
6oz (170g) fresh goats' milk
6oz (170g) distilled or spring water
4oz (113g) sodium hydroxide (caustic soda/lye)
2 tsp (10g) bay essential oil
1 tsp (5g) pine essential oil
1 tsp (5g) rosewood essential oil

Grease a shallow square or oblong mould. Place the olive oil and beeswax in a stainless steel or enamel pot over a low heat. Heat the milk to room temperature. Pour the water and the milk into a heavy glass or plastic bowl or jug. Wearing rubber gloves and eye protection, add the sodium hydroxide to the liquid and stir until dissolved. When the oils have melted, remove them from the heat.

Place one sugar thermometer in the oils and one in the caustic solution. When both thermometers reach an equal temperature between 120°F (49°C) and 140°F (60°C), pour the caustic solution into the oil. Stir occasionally until the mixture reaches trace. This should take about 20 minutes.

Add the essential oils and stir well. Pour immediately into the mould and cover with a towel or blanket. Leave to set for 24 hours or until the soap reaches a solid consistency. Wearing rubber gloves, remove the soap from the mould and cut into bars. Cover the soap and leave to cure for four weeks before use.

olive splendour

This soap contains kelp or powdered seaweed, which gives it a nice, speckled effect and a smooth texture. Kelp is packed with vitamins and minerals, and when added to oodles of wonderful olive oil it results in a soap that is somewhat splendid! I've used a cedarwood fragrance oil to give the bar a warm, woody scent.

soap style:
- ❏ hard bar with rich, creamy lather
- ❏ good for all skin types

30oz (849g) olive oil
2oz (57g) beeswax
10oz (283g) distilled or spring water
4oz (113g) sodium hydroxide (caustic soda/lye)
1 tbsp (15g) powdered kelp
2 tsp (10g) cedarwood fragrance oil
1 tsp (5g) diluted chromium oxide (green)

Grease an oblong, square or shaped mould. Place the oil and beeswax in a stainless steel or enamel pot over a low heat. Pour the water into a heavy glass or plastic bowl or jug. Wearing rubber gloves and eye protection, add the sodium hydroxide to the water and stir until dissolved. When the wax has melted, remove it from the heat.

Place one sugar thermometer in the oils and one in the caustic solution. When both thermometers reach an equal temperature between 120°F (49°C) and 140°F (60°C), pour the caustic solution into the oil. Stir occasionally until the mixture reaches trace. This should take about 40 minutes.

Sprinkle the kelp into the mixture, add the fragrance oil and diluted colouring and stir well. Pour immediately into the mould and cover with a towel or blanket. Leave to set for 24 hours or until the soap reaches a solid consistency. Wearing rubber gloves, remove the soap from the moulds and trim to shape. Cover the soap and leave to cure for four weeks before use.

glycerine soaps

Every soaper dreams of making a clear soap, but sadly this is easier said than done. The best I have achieved is a cloudy soap with a high gloss. Clear soap depends on a good, basic soap recipe and the addition of solvents. These solvents include sugar, glycerine and alcohol, and it is obtaining the alcohol that has caused the most problems. The best alcohol you can use for transparent soap is called ethanol, impossible to buy in the UK. One alternative is isopropyl, or rubbing alcohol. This smells like methylated spirits and is very costly. At the time of writing, Butterbur and Sage (see Stockists on page 79) are in the process of obtaining a licence to sell de-natured alcohol. This should provide a solution to the problem.

For the purposes of this book, I have used both 80%-proof vodka and whisky. Even when using these spirits in your recipe you are not guaranteed perfect results. Mine are illustrated here but I got through two bottles of vodka and a bottle of whisky before the results were pleasing enough to present to you.

I give my recipe and method below, but for those who are intent on exploring the possibilities, I recommend a book solely on the subject of transparent soapmaking in Further Reading (see page 79).

If you are more interested in the creative results than the homespun processes, you can buy ready-made clear glycerine soap compound from several suppliers in the UK, and this is the stuff I used to produce my blue angels (overleaf). The method is very simple – you melt down the soap compound, add colourants and/or fragrances and pour it into a mould. The cost is minimal, especially when compared to the cost of whisky, and you have the added advantage of leaving your soapmaking session in an upright and sober condition.

glycerine soap

basic recipe

14oz (397g) dripping (tallow)
8oz (227g) coconut oil
6oz (170g) olive oil
4oz (113g) castor oil
11oz (312g) distilled or spring water
4½oz (127g) sodium hydroxide (caustic soda/lye)
fragrance oil of your choice

additional ingredients required to make the soap clear

2oz (57g) granulated sugar
3oz (85g) distilled or spring water
2oz (57g) glycerine
4oz (113g) whisky or vodka
wax chip colouring of your choice
fragrance oil of your choice

CAUTIONARY NOTE: Alcohol is extremely flammable. Work on an electric rather than a gas ring and have a fire extinguisher or some wet towels to hand.

Following the basic recipe, place the fat and oils in a stainless steel or enamel pot over a low heat. Pour the water into a heavy glass or plastic bowl or jug. Wearing

I have used latex cherubs which were designed for plaster-casting. A wide variety of alternative moulds is available from glycerine soap suppliers and you will find details in the list of Stockists (see page 79).

out 8oz (227g) of the powdered soap. Place this in a double-boiler or in a bowl in a pan of boiling water. During the following process keep the water in the pan at a steady bubble, adding more water to the base pan if the level gets low. Add 2oz (57g) of water from the second list of ingredients, plus the glycerine, to the grated soap.

Cover the bowl and leave the soap to melt, pushing it down with a spatula from time to time but not too hard as you want to avoid creating any foam. After about 45 minutes the soap will turn to gel. At this stage, heat up the remaining water and pour it into the bowl of sugar, then stir until the sugar dissolves. Add the alcohol to the soap mix and cover it. Stir gently from time to time but keep the pot covered as much as possible to avoid evaporation. After 10 minutes, add the sugar solution to the soap and alcohol and stir. The soap will gradually reduce to syrup, which can take up to 45 minutes. Take the wax colour chips and, with a sharp knife, make some shavings and add them to the soap. Only a couple of small shavings are needed to colour this quantity of soap. Add a few more drops of fragrance or essential oil if required. Stir enough to dissolve the colour chips but do this with care. When the soap is completely liquid, pour it into moulds through a sieve. Immediately place the moulds in a freezer and leave for an hour or until solid. Remove from the freezer and turn out the soap. Leave to cure for two weeks before use.

instant glycerine soap

If you are using ready-made glycerine soap, this should be placed in a double-boiler and will melt within 5 or 10 minutes. Add the colouring (wax chips, food or soap colouring), add a few drops of fragrance oil and stir. Pour the melted soap directly into the mould of your choice. Leave the soap to set overnight and remove from the moulds. This soap can be used immediately.

rubber gloves and eye protection, add the sodium hydroxide to the water and stir until dissolved. When the oils have melted, remove them from the heat.

Place one sugar thermometer in the oils and one in the caustic solution. When both thermometers reach an equal temperature between 120°F (49°C) and 140°F (60°C), pour the caustic solution into the oil. (See pages 31-32 for more information.) Stir occasionally until the mixture reaches trace. This should take about 25 minutes.

At trace, add the fragrance oil and stir well. Pour immediately into the mould and cover with a towel or blanket. Leave to set for 24 hours or until the soap reaches a solid consistency. Wearing rubber gloves, turn the soap out of the mould and cut into chunks. Cover the soap and leave to cure for two weeks.

Place the sugar in a bowl and set aside. With a cheese-grater, grate the soap as finely as you can and weigh

creamy coconut soaps

In my opinion, coconut oil makes the loveliest soaps. Some consider it to be a little drying on the skin but all the soaps I have made containing this oil have been rich in large, creamy bubbles and have certainly not troubled my very sensitive skin. Soap made entirely from coconut oil is particularly useful for beach holidays because this is the only oil that will lather in salt water. You can make 16oz (454g) of pure coconut oil soap using 16oz (454g) coconut oil, 3oz (85g) sodium hydroxide (caustic soda/lye) and 8¾oz (247g) distilled or spring water, but you may find the resulting soap looks somewhat grainy. In the following recipes I have balanced the oils to achieve quite gentle soaps which I hope you will enjoy making and using.

coconut ice

Be careful to keep this soap away from the kids as the resemblance to its sweet namesake could result in a mouth full of bubbles and a lifetime's aversion to coconut. Although it is quite time-consuming to prepare, you will find the end result is a pleasure to use and well worth the effort.

soap style:
- ❏ good antiseptic qualities
- ❏ great for greasy skin
- ❏ hard soap with large bubbles

11oz (312g) vegetable fat (shortening)
21oz (594g) coconut oil
15¾oz (446g) distilled or spring water
5½oz (156g) sodium hydroxide (caustic soda/lye)
2 tsp (10g) geranium essential oil
2 tsp (10g) rose fragrance oil
2 tsp (10g) diluted cosmetic pigment (D&C red 28)

There is no colouring in the first batch and it should be set aside for two weeks before making the second (pink) batch.

Grease a shallow square or oblong mould. Place the fat and oil in a stainless steel or enamel pot over a low heat. Pour the water into a heavy glass or plastic bowl or jug. Wearing

> **g**eraniums are available in numerous delicious varieties. Their wonderful fragrant leaves have an incredible range of scents including apple, apricot, chocolate mint, cinnamon rose, coconut, ginger, lavender, lemon, nutmeg, old spice, peppermint, champagne, rose and strawberry. You can infuse any of these leaves in olive oil and add them to your soap (see pages 30-31).

rubber gloves and eye protection, add the sodium hydroxide (caustic soda/lye) to the water and stir until dissolved. When the oils have melted, remove them from the heat.

Place one sugar thermometer in the oils and one in the caustic solution. When both thermometers reach an equal temperature between 120°F (49°C) and 140°F (60°C), pour the caustic solution into the oil. (See pages 31-32 for more information.) Stir occasionally until the mixture reaches trace. This should take about 40 minutes.

Add the essential oils and stir well. Pour immediately into the mould to a depth of ½in (12mm) and cover with a towel or blanket. Put to one side and leave for two weeks.

After two weeks, make a second batch of soap using the same recipe as for the first batch, and proceed until you reach trace. At this point, dissolve ¼ tsp (1g) of red pigment in 2 tsp (10g) of warm water and stir thoroughly. Add the diluted pigment to the soap a few drops at a time, stirring continuously. When the soap has turned bright red pour it over the set white soap, to a depth of

tip

*i*f you have a problem releasing the soap, place the moulds in the freezer for an hour. Take them out and let them sit for 10 minutes, then turn them upside down and tap the top of each one lightly until the soap falls out.

½in (12mm). Don't worry if the new soap trickles over the edges of the white soap as this can be trimmed later. Leave for 24 hours or until hard. Wearing rubber gloves, remove both layers of soap from the mould and cut into equal-sized blocks. Cover the soap and leave to cure for four weeks before use.

coconut cream soap

The inclusion of cocoa butter in this recipe results in a wonderfully hard but gentle batch of soap that is ideal for fancy-shaped moulds. I have scented this soap with rosewood essential oil, my personal favourite. Sadly, the use of rosewood is not environmentally sound so those with a deep-rooted ecological conscience might prefer to use howood or holeaf.

soap style:
❏ hard but creamy soap with large bubbles
❏ good for all skin types

24oz (680g) coconut oil
8oz (227g) cocoa butter
16oz (454g) distilled or spring water
5¾oz (163g) sodium hydroxide (caustic soda/lye)
2 tsp (10g) essential oils such as rosewood, howood
 or holeaf

Grease a shallow square or oblong mould with vegetable fat and make the soap according to the basic Coconut Ice instructions above. It will take approximately 30 minutes to reach trace. Add the essential oils and stir well. Pour immediately into the mould and cover with a towel or blanket. Leave to set for 24 hours or until the soap reaches a solid consistency. Wearing rubber gloves, remove the soap from the mould. If you have used a slab mould or a PVC pipe, cut the soap into bars at this stage. Cover the soap and leave to cure for four weeks before use.

antiseptic soaps

There are many different reasons for selecting a particular soap. Sometimes we choose one to pamper and perfume, sometimes to clean and scrub, and sometimes to refresh us so we can begin the day with a zing rather than a flop. The following soaps have specific purposes and are guaranteed to do the job for which they are intended. There was a time when a soap had to smell strongly antiseptic before we were convinced that it was actually getting us clean, and I suspect many readers may look back and remember such brands with some affection. Here are my replacements for carbolic and the like, which I offer in the hope that you will find them welcome and useful additions to your soap wardrobe.

magic soap

Believe it or not, this soap was coloured with bright blue cosmetic pigment. As you can see, it turned bright fuchsia although there are still some patches of blue on the bars. The speckles are the result of the grey cosmetic clay.

soap style:
- ❏ hard with large bubbles
- ❏ decorative hand soap

12oz (340g) dripping (tallow)
18oz (510g) coconut oil
2oz (57g) almond oil
12oz (340g) distilled or spring water
5oz (142g) sodium hydroxide (caustic soda/lye)
2 tsp (10g) grey cosmetic clay
1 tsp (5g) castor oil
1 tsp (5g) tea tree essential oil
1 tbsp (15g) lavender essential oil
1 tbsp (15g) diluted bright blue cosmetic
    pigment (309009)

Grease a square mould. Place the fat and base oils in a stainless steel or enamel pot over a low heat. Pour the water into a heavy glass or plastic bowl or jug. Wearing rubber gloves and eye protection, add the sodium hydroxide to the water and stir until dissolved. When the oils have melted, remove them from the heat.

Place one sugar thermometer in the oils and one in the caustic solution. When both thermometers reach an equal temperature between 120°F (49°C) and 140°F (60°C), pour the caustic solution into the oil. (See pages 31-32 for more information.) Stir occasionally until the mixture reaches trace. This should take about 45 minutes.

Sprinkle the clay into the mix and stir well. Add the castor and essential oils and then add the diluted colouring. Stir well. Pour immediately into the mould and cover with a towel or blanket. Leave to set for 24 hours or until the soap reaches a solid consistency. Wearing rubber gloves, remove the soap from the mould and cut into bars. Cover the soap and leave to cure for four weeks.

gardener's soap

This soap has a scrubby texture and makes use of the antiseptic qualities of tea tree and eucalyptus essential oils. This combination of oils is balanced by gentle carrot root oil. This is the soap you should use to remove the mud and slugs from your hands after a hard day's gardening.

soap style:
❑ very hard with large bubbles
❑ good for all skin types but primarily a hand soap

10oz (283g) vegetable fat (shortening)
8oz (227g) coconut oil
8oz (227g) palm oil
6oz (170g) olive oil

14oz (397g) distilled or spring water

5oz (142g) sodium hydroxide (caustic soda/lye)

1 tbsp (15g) powdered pumice

1 tbsp (15g) carrot root oil

1 tbsp (15g) each of tea tree and eucalyptus essential oils

Grease a shallow square or oblong mould. Place the fat and base oils in a stainless steel or enamel pot over a low heat. Pour the water and into a heavy glass or plastic bowl or jug. Wearing rubber gloves and eye protection, add the sodium hydroxide (caustic soda/lye) to the water and stir until dissolved. When the oils have melted, remove them from the heat.

Place one sugar thermometer in the oils and one in the caustic solution. When both thermometers reach an equal temperature between 120°F (49°C) and 140°F (60°C), pour the caustic solution into the oil. (See pages 31-32 for more information.) Stir occasionally until the mixture reaches trace. This should take about 60 minutes.

Sprinkle the pumice into the mix and stir well. Add the carrot and essential oils and stir well. Pour immediately into the mould and cover with a towel or blanket. Leave to set for 24 hours or until the soap reaches a solid consistency.

Wearing rubber gloves, remove the soap from the mould and cut into bars. Cover the soap and leave to cure for four weeks before use.

buzz off

Both citronella and lavender act as wonderful insect-repellents so this soap will definitely keep the bugs at bay. For extra protection put one part glycerine and four parts water into a spray bottle and add a few drops of these essential oils. If you don't have glycerine to hand, use straight vodka as a base instead. If you don't have citronella, lemon grass is equally effective.

soap style:

- ❏ medium soap with medium bubbles
- ❏ refreshing
- ❏ good for all skin types

12oz (340g) vegetable fat (shortening)

12oz (340g) coconut oil

8oz (227g) olive oil

11oz (312g) distilled or spring water

5oz (142g) sodium hydroxide (caustic soda/lye)

1 tbsp (15g) lavender essential oil

2 tsp (10g) citronella essential oil

Grease a square or oblong mould. Place the fat and base oils in a stainless steel or enamel pot over a low heat. Pour the water into a heavy glass or plastic bowl or jug. Wearing rubber gloves and eye protection, add the sodium hydroxide (caustic soda/lye) to the water and stir until dissolved. When the oils have melted, remove them from the heat.

Place one sugar thermometer in the oils and one in the caustic solution. When both thermometers reach an equal temperature between 120°F (49°C) and 140°F (60°C), pour the caustic solution into the oil. (See pages 31-32 for more information.) Stir occasionally until the mixture reaches trace. This should take about 60 minutes.

Add the essential oils and stir well. Pour immediately into the mould and cover with a towel or blanket. Leave to set for 24 hours or until the soap reaches a solid consistency. Wearing rubber gloves, remove the soap from the mould and cut into bars. Cover the soap and leave to cure for four weeks before use.

soaps for the life
in your man

For my female readers, here is your opportunity to create the man of your dreams. Clean him up with a bar of Scrub-A-Dub or make him kissable with delicious Vanilla Delight. Just for once, you can compose a fragrance that you truly like rather than have his choice imposed upon you. One missing element from this section is a good shaving soap. This is because traditional, soft shaving soaps are made with potassium hydroxide which is extremely difficult for the home soaper to obtain. As an alternative, use the Olive Splendour recipe on page 54 and add 1oz (28g) of glycerine, lanolin or castor oil at trace. Choose essential oils with antiseptic qualities and, if you want to be really kind to his skin, add a little comfrey for its healing qualities.

scrub-a-dub

This is a lovely, scrubby soap with a fresh, forest scent and a smart grey-green colour. Green clay draws the grime out of the skin so this is the soap to use after a hard day's work.

soap style:
- ❏ hard, large bubbles
- ❏ lovely, smooth texture

12oz (340g) dripping (tallow)
8oz (227g) sunflower oil
12oz (340g) coconut oil
1oz (28g) beeswax
11½oz (325g) distilled or spring water
5oz (142g) sodium hydroxide (caustic soda/lye)
1 tsp (5g) diluted chromium oxide (green)
2 tbsp (30g) green cosmetic clay
2 tsp (10g) sandalwood essential oil
2 tsp (10g) pine essential oil

Grease a shallow square or oblong mould. Place the fat, base oils and beeswax in a stainless steel or enamel pot over a low heat. Pour the water into a heavy glass or plastic bowl or jug. Wearing rubber gloves and eye protection, add the sodium hydroxide (caustic soda/lye) to the water and stir until dissolved. When the oils have melted, remove them from the heat.

Place one sugar thermometer in the oils and one in the caustic solution. When both thermometers reach an equal temperature between 120°F (49°C) and 140°F (60°C), pour the caustic solution into the oil. (See pages 31-32 for more information.) Stir occasionally until the mixture reaches trace. This should take about 30 minutes.

As the mixture thickens, just before trace, add the colouring, sprinkle in the clay and stir well. At trace, add the essential oils and stir again. Pour immediately into the mould and cover with a towel or blanket. Leave to set for 24 hours or until the soap reaches a solid consistency. Wearing rubber gloves, remove the soap from the mould and cut into bars. Cover the soap and leave to cure for four weeks before use.

spicy mint big boy

This is a good basic recipe, with a spicy, minty fragrance. I have coloured the batch with paprika but you could replace this with cinnamon. For a mould I used a short section of drainpipe that my plumber was kind enough to leave lying about. One of these days I'm going to get myself arrested for mould theft!

soap style:
- ❏ slightly grainy but hard with medium bubbles
- ❏ not for very sensitive skins

scrub-a-dub (left), vanilla delight (right), spicy mint big boy (bottom)

12oz (340g) vegetable fat (shortening)

8oz (227g) lard

12oz (340g) coconut oil

2oz (57g) beeswax

11½oz (325g) distilled or spring water

5oz (142g) sodium hydroxide (caustic soda/lye)

1 tbsp (15g) powdered paprika

1 tsp (5g) each peppermint and ginger essential oils

2 tsp (10g) cinnamon essential oil

Grease a shallow square or oblong mould. Place the fats, base oil and beeswax in a stainless steel or enamel pot over a low heat. Pour the water into a heavy glass or plastic bowl or jug. Wearing rubber gloves and eye protection, add the sodium hydroxide (lye) to the water and stir until dissolved. When the oils have melted, remove them from the heat.

Place one sugar thermometer in the oils and one in the caustic solution. When both thermometers reach an equal temperature between 120°F (49°C) and 140°F (60°C), pour the caustic solution into the oil. (See pages 31-32 for more information.) Stir occasionally until the mixture reaches trace. This should take about 10 minutes.

Just before trace, sprinkle in the paprika and stir thoroughly. At trace, add the essential oils and stir again. Pour immediately into the mould and cover with a towel or blanket. Leave to set for 24 hours or until the soap reaches a solid consistency. Wearing rubber gloves, remove the soap from the mould and cut into bars. Cover the soap and leave to cure for four weeks before use.

vanilla delight

Vanilla is absolutely delicious in soap. There is no true vanilla essential oil, although you can buy an absolute oil for a small fortune. There are various diluted substitutes being sold as essential oils and you can also find vanilla fragrance oils to use in your soaps. While I list this as a man's soap, that is more wishful thinking than fact.

soap style:
- ❏ hard bar with medium bubbles
- ❏ very yummy

24oz (680g) vegetable fat (shortening)

8oz (227g) coconut oil

2oz (57g) beeswax

11oz (312g) distilled or spring water

5oz (142g) sodium hydroxide (caustic soda/lye)

4 tsp (20g) vanilla fragrance oil

Grease a shallow square or oblong mould. Place the fat, base oil and beeswax in a stainless steel or enamel pot over a low heat. Pour the water into a heavy glass or plastic bowl or jug. Wearing rubber gloves and eye protection, add the sodium hydroxide (caustic soda/lye) to the water and stir until dissolved. When the oils have melted, remove them from the heat.

Place one sugar thermometer in the oils and one in the caustic solution. When both thermometers reach an equal temperature between 120°F (49°C) and 140°F (60°C), pour the caustic solution into the oil. Stir occasionally until the mixture reaches trace. This should take about 25 minutes.

At trace, add the fragrance oil and stir well. Pour immediately into the mould and cover with a towel or blanket. Leave to set for 24 hours or until the soap reaches a solid consistency. Wearing rubber gloves, remove the soap from the mould and cut into bars. Cover the soap and leave to cure for four weeks before use.

special editions

All the soaps in this section have special uses and make ideal gifts for special people. Include the Kitchen Soap in a basket with fresh herbs and spices, or pack the Baby Soap with some rubber ducks or other baby bathtime accessories. The Mystic Soap was moulded in a large PVC pipe and the centre was cut out just as the soap began to harden. Hand Maiden is a lovely winter soap, so pack it together with some lip balm and, perhaps, a pair of woolly gloves. Make the Sunshine Soap for a summer gift or use it to brighten a collection of uncoloured soaps. Green Machine is ideal for vegetarians.

kitchen soap

Here is a great bar of soap that will remove the smell of onions and garlic from your hands. The secret is the inclusion of fresh coffee, which also gives the soap an interesting speckled appearance. Grind your coffee finely before brewing.

soap style:
- ❑ hard and creamy with large bubbles
- ❑ good for all skin types

2 tbsp (30g) fresh coffee grounds
11½oz (325g) distilled or spring water
12oz (340g) dripping (tallow)
12oz (340g) coconut oil
8oz (227g) olive oil
5oz (142g) sodium hydroxide (caustic soda/lye)

Grease a square or oblong mould. Place the coffee grounds in a heavy glass or plastic bowl or jug, boil up the water and pour it over the coffee. Stir it, then leave to become completely cold.

Place the fat and base oils in a stainless steel or enamel pot over a low heat. Wearing rubber gloves and eye protection, add the sodium hydroxide (caustic soda/lye) to the brewed coffee and stir until dissolved. When the oils have melted, remove them from the heat.

Place one sugar thermometer in the oils and one in the caustic solution. When both thermometers reach an equal temperature between 120°F (49°C) and 140°F (60°C), pour the caustic solution into the oil. Stir occasionally until the mixture reaches trace. This should take about 25 minutes.

Pour immediately into the mould and cover with a towel or blanket. Leave to set for 24 hours or until the soap reaches a solid consistency. Wearing rubber gloves, remove the soap from the mould and cut into blocks. Cover the soap and leave to cure for four weeks before use.

baby soap

Here is a really gentle soap that's safe for baby and for those with very sensitive skins. I've left it uncoloured and unperfumed. For a healing soap you might consider replacing the calendula-infused oil with an oil infused with comfrey. This is particularly good for use on bruised or cut skin.

soap style:
- ❏ very mild and gentle
- ❏ medium texture with small creamy bubbles
- ❏ perfect for sensitive skins

8oz (227g) vegetable fat (shortening)
8oz (227g) calendula-infused sweet almond oil (see pages 22-3)
8oz (227g) sunflower oil
8oz (227g) coconut oil
2oz (57g) white beeswax
11oz (312g) distilled or spring water
5oz (142g) sodium hydroxide (caustic soda/lye)
1 tsp (5g) carrot seed oil

Grease your chosen moulds. Place the fat, base oils and beeswax in a stainless steel or enamel pot over a low heat. Pour the water into a heavy glass or plastic bowl or jug. Wearing rubber gloves and eye protection, add the sodium hydroxide (caustic soda/lye) to the water and stir until dissolved. When the oils have melted, remove them from the heat.

Place one sugar thermometer in the oils and one in the caustic solution. When both thermometers reach an equal temperature between 120°F (49°C) and 140°F (60°C), pour the caustic solution into the oil. (See pages 31-32 for more information.) Stir occasionally until the mixture reaches trace. This should take about 90 minutes.

Add the carrot seed oil and stir well. Pour immediately into the moulds and cover with a towel or blanket. Leave to set for 24 hours or until the soap reaches a solid consistency. Wearing rubber gloves, remove the soap from the moulds. Cover the soap and leave to cure for six weeks before use.

sunshine soap

This pretty, yellow soap is cheap to produce and has a nicely hard consistency. I've perfumed it with a daffodil fragrance oil but if you prefer to use essential oils you could try a blend of camomile and lemon.

soap style:
- ❏ hard soap with large bubbles
- ❏ pretty addition to a gift basket

6oz (170g) lard
12oz (340g) coconut oil
12oz (340g) sunflower oil
10½oz (297g) distilled or spring water
5oz (142g) sodium hydroxide (caustic soda/lye)
1 tbsp (15g) fragrance oil
2 tsp (10g) diluted yellow cosmetic pigment (FD&C yellow 5)

Grease your chosen moulds. Place the fat and base oils in a stainless steel or enamel pot over a low heat. Set aside ½oz (14g) of the water and pour the remainder into a heavy glass or plastic bowl or jug. Wearing rubber gloves and eye protection, add the sodium hydroxide (caustic soda/lye) to the water and stir until dissolved. When the oils have melted, remove them from the heat.

Place one sugar thermometer in the oils and one in the caustic solution. When both thermometers reach an equal temperature between 120°F (49°C) and 140°F (60°C), pour the caustic solution into the oil. (See pages 31-32 for more information.) Stir occasionally until the mixture reaches trace. This should take about 90 minutes.

Add the fragrance oil and stir well. Then stir in the cosmetic colouring. Pour immediately into the moulds and cover with a towel or blanket. Leave to set for 24 hours or until the soap reaches a solid consistency. Wearing rubber gloves, remove the soap from the moulds. Cover the soap and leave to cure for four weeks before use.

mystic soap

If you are over 40, this soap will take you back to the 1960s when patchouli was the only scent to wear. I used blue cosmetic pigment in this soap and it turned a deep shade of violet. It fades to a very pale and pretty lavender once the soap had cured (photograph appears on page 76).

soap style:
❑ medium/hard with medium bubbles

12oz (340g) vegetable fat (shortening)
10oz (283g) dripping (tallow)
8oz (227g) olive oil
9oz (255g) distilled or spring water

4oz (113g) sodium hydroxide (caustic soda/lye)
1 tbsp (15g) patchouli essential oil
1 tsp (5g) lavender essential oil
1 tbsp (15g) diluted cosmetic pigment (FD&C blue 1)

Grease your chosen moulds. Place the fats and base oil in a stainless steel or enamel pot over a low heat. Pour the water into a heavy glass or plastic bowl or jug. Wearing rubber gloves and eye protection, add the sodium hydroxide (lye) to the water and stir until dissolved. When the oils have melted, remove them from the heat.

Place one sugar thermometer in the oils and one in the caustic solution. When both thermometers reach an equal

baby soap (top), sunshine soap (centre), green machine (bottom), handmaiden (heart)

temperature between 120°F (49°C) and 140°F (60°C), pour the caustic solution into the oil. (See pages 31-32 for more information.) Stir occasionally until the mixture reaches trace. This should take about 90 minutes.

Add the essential oils and diluted pigment and stir well. Pour immediately into the moulds and cover with a towel or blanket. Leave to set for 24 hours or until the soap reaches a solid consistency. Wearing rubber gloves, remove the soap from the moulds. Cover the soap and leave to cure for four weeks before use.

hand maiden

This is a kind hand soap containing lanolin which protects the skin and is particularly useful for chapped hands. Some people are allergic to lanolin so always make the recipient of your soap fully aware of all the ingredients to avoid any unpleasant or unfortunate consequences.

soap style:
- ❏ creamy
- ❏ hard with medium bubbles

12oz (340g) dripping (tallow)
12oz (340g) coconut oil
8oz (227g) sunflower oil
11oz (312g) distilled or spring water
5oz (142g) sodium hydroxide (caustic soda/lye)
2 heaped tbsp (40g) dried comfrey
1 tbsp (15g) ylang-ylang essential oil
1 tsp (5g) camomile essential oil
1 tbsp (15g) lanolin
1 tsp (5g) diluted ultramarine rose pigment

Grease your chosen moulds. Place the fat and base oils in a stainless steel or enamel pot over a low heat. Pour the water into a heavy glass or plastic bowl or jug. Wearing rubber gloves and eye protection, add the sodium hydroxide (caustic soda/lye) to the water and stir until dissolved. When the oils have melted, remove them from the heat.

Place one sugar thermometer in the oils and one in the caustic solution. When both thermometers reach an equal temperature between 120°F (49°C) and 140°F (60°C), pour the caustic solution into the oil. (See pages 31-32 for more information.) Stir occasionally until the mixture reaches trace. This should take about 90 minutes.

Scatter the comfrey into the mix and stir. Stir in the essential oils and lanolin. Then add the colouring and stir again. Pour immediately into the moulds and cover with a towel or blanket. Leave to set for 24 hours or until the soap reaches a solid consistency. Wearing rubber gloves, remove the soap from the moulds. Cover the soap and leave to cure for four weeks before use.

green machine

This recipe is good for vegetarians and produces a good basic bar of soap that reacts well to coloured pigments. It also contains kaolin, which gives the soap a really smooth texture.

soap style:
- ❏ hard with medium bubbles

10oz (283g) vegetable fat (shortening)
12oz (340g) coconut oil
10oz (283g) corn oil
11½oz (325g) distilled or spring water
5oz (142g) sodium hydroxide (caustic soda/lye)
2 tbsp (30g) lime essential oil
2 tbsp (30g) kaolin
2 tsp (10g) diluted cosmetic pigment (D&C green 5)

Grease your chosen moulds. Place the fats and base oils in a stainless steel or enamel pot over a low heat. Pour the water into a heavy glass or plastic bowl or jug. Wearing rubber gloves and eye protection, add the sodium hydroxide (caustic soda/lye) to the water and stir until dissolved. When the oils have melted, remove them from the heat.

Place one sugar thermometer in the oils and one in the caustic solution. When both thermometers reach an equal temperature between 120°F (49°C) and 140°F (60°C), pour the caustic solution into the oil. (See pages 31-32 for more information.) Stir occasionally until the mixture reaches trace. This should take about 90 minutes.

Sprinkle in the kaolin, add the essential oil and diluted pigment and stir well. Pour immediately into the moulds and cover with a towel or blanket. Leave to set for 24 hours or until the soap reaches a solid consistency. Wearing rubber gloves, remove the soap from the moulds. Cover the soap and leave to cure for four weeks before use.

bathtime luxuries

There is nothing so relaxing as wallowing in a sweetly-scented hot bath, and here are a few extra luxuries for your sensual delight. Package them cleverly and give them as gifts to accessorize your soaps or use them to pamper yourself after a hard day at the soap pot. One recipe here that you must try is the Lush Floating Bath Soak. It leaves your skin feeling so soft that you will never want to be without it. Here, also, you can put your skills at blending fragrant oils to the test as there is no sodium hydroxide (caustic soda/lye) to distort the final effect. During the summer months be sure to pick, and dry, sweet-smelling flowers and herbs for use in your recipes.

bath grains

bath bags

Little muslin bath bags are great for exfoliating the skin and are a pretty addition to a gift basket. You can make them very easily using a base of your favourite grated soap, dried herbs and flower petals, and a finely-ground grain such as cornmeal. The bags can be rubbed directly on your skin or hung from a ribbon under the bath tap.

basic ingredients
8oz (227g) grated soap (use one containing essential oils)
2oz (57g) cornmeal
2oz (57g) oatmeal
1oz (28g) ground almonds (almond meal)

astringent
½ tsp (2.5g) lavender flowers
½ tsp (2.5g) fresh rosemary leaves
1 drop camomile essential oil

sweet and fresh
½ tsp (2.5g) finely powdered, dried, orange and
   lemon peel
1 tsp (5g) dried rose petals
1 drop geranium essential oil

gentle and soothing
½ tsp (2.5g) dried calendula petals
½ tsp (2.5g) grated cocoa butter
4 drops of wheatgerm oil

Mix the basic ingredients with one of the bath bag combinations. With pinking shears, cut out a 6-in (15 cm) square of white muslin (cheesecloth). Place 1 tbsp (15g) of the mixture in the centre of the square, draw up the corners of the muslin to form a bag and secure with a length of colourfast narrow satin ribbon or raffia.

bath grains

The contents of the bath bags can be poured directly into your bath water where they will act as a softening agent. You can display them in decorative bottles and add some extra flower petals and/or leaves to add to the overall effect. The addition of a teaspoonful per bottle of large grained sea salt, will make for a very relaxing bath.

milk and rose bath

This is for those who want to luxuriate for hours in a moisturizing, wildly decadent tub of lovelies.

1oz (28g) cocoa butter
6 drops of rose fragrance
1oz (28g) finely-grated soap
6oz (170g) powdered milk
1 tbsp (15g) cream of tartar
1 tbsp (15g) cornmeal (cornstarch)

Put the cocoa butter in a double-boiler over a low heat until melted. Add the rose fragrance, then pour into an ice-cube container. Place in the freezer and leave to set hard. Remove from the container and grate very finely. Mix, either by hand or in a food-processor, with the other ingredients. Add 2-3 tbsp (30-45g) per bath.

bath fizzies

These little blocks of fun fizz in the bath and the cocoa butter acts as a good moisturizer.

2oz (57g) cocoa butter
2oz (57g) bicarbonate of soda
1oz (28g) citric acid
3 tbsp (45g) cornmeal (cornstarch)
6 drops of diluted cosmetic pigment or food colouring of
   your choice
6 drops of essential oil of your choice

Grease some small moulds or an ice-cube tray with non-stick cooking spray. Melt the cocoa butter in a double-boiler over a low heat. Remove from the heat, add the bicarbonate of soda, citric acid and cornmeal (cornstarch) and stir thoroughly. Add the drops of colouring and essential oil and stir. Spoon into moulds and place in the freezer to set. When hard, turn out of the moulds.

Lush floating bath soak

This recipe was donated by Lush, who are to the bath what The Body Shop are to the body. Read about Lush on page 7, but for now just give this recipe a try and you are in for a thoroughly relaxing bathtime experience.

left to right:
layered bath oil, splish splash,
bath fizzies, milk and rose bath

3oz (85g) cocoa butter
$\frac{1}{4}$oz (7g) fresh banana
1 tsp (5g) olive oil
1 tbsp (15g) creamed coconut
1 tbsp (15g) honey
1 tbsp (15g) fresh or desiccated coconut
2 drops tangerine essential oil

Mix all the ingredients, except the essential oil, in a pan and warm gently. Remove from the heat and leave to cool for a few minutes, then stir in the essential oil. Pour into an ice-cube tray or a similar flexible mould. Put into the refrigerator and leave overnight to set. Add a chunk – about 1oz (28g) – to the bath water as the taps start running. Relax and let the oils soften your skin.

layered bath oil

This is a pretty addition to any bathroom and you can use colourings to match your scent. Try peppermint essential oil with green colouring or strawberry fragrance oil with red colouring. Don't add too much colouring or you will end up with dyed bathwater and towels. Use sparingly as too much will leave a film on your skin.

4 drops liquid food colouring
2oz (57g) distilled or spring water
4 drops essential or fragrance oil
2oz (57g) almond oil

Add the colouring to the water and the essential or fragrance oil to the almond oil. Pour the coloured water into a clear glass bottle, then pour the perfumed almond oil on top.

splish, splash

This refreshing toner is great for your face. You can replace the orange flower water with rosewater if you wish.

2oz (57g) orange flower water
1oz (28g) witch hazel
1 tbsp (15g) glycerine
2 tsp (10g) vodka
10 drops ylang-ylang essential oil
10 drops lemon essential oil

Put all the ingredients into a narrow-necked glass bottle and shake thoroughly.

hair care

All the soaps in this book can be used as shampoos, although it is best to avoid those that include colouring agents. It is also wise to use a slightly acidic rinse following the shampoo to restore the natural acid balance of the hair. Something as simple as 1 tbsp (15g) of fresh lemon juice or cider vinegar diluted in 1 pint ($\frac{1}{2}$ litre) of water will do the trick, or you can try the Parsley and Lemon Hair Rinse recipe included here.

For a truly natural shampoo solution you can use an infusion of soapwort leaves and roots together with any of the herbs listed above. Although you will not achieve a rich lather, soapwort does produce mild suds and has good cleansing properties. Use 1oz (28g) of either fresh or dried soapwort together with $\frac{1}{2}$oz (14g) of the herb of your choice. Put these in a saucepan with 1 pint ($\frac{1}{2}$ litre) of boiling water and simmer for 15 minutes. Set aside for another 40 minutes, strain the liquid from the herbs and the shampoo is ready to use. Unfortunately this shampoo cannot be stored so you will need to make a fresh solution for each application. Your dog can also benefit from your soapmaking. Try using the Buzz Off soap on page 61 as a dog shampoo – it will help to keep the fleas at bay.

In my experience, soaps containing high levels of olive oil make the best shampoo bars. They produce a rich, creamy lather with very little rubbing and leave the hair silky-soft. Adding a couple of tablespoonfuls of castor oil to a recipe containing plenty of coconut oil will also result in a silky-smooth shampoo bar with lots of bubbles.

Many herbs can be used to enhance the colour and/or texture of your hair and these can be added in various ways to your shampoo bar. Infuse selected herbs in your base oils or liquidize fresh herbs and add them to the water content of your soap. Here is a list of ingredients, compiled by Elaya Tsosie, that you may wish to incorporate according to your needs:

BURDOCK: Root helps to prevent dandruff.

CAMOMILE: Softens and lightens hair.

CATMINT: Encourages hair growth and soothes scalps.

FLANNEL MULLEIN: Flowers lighten hair.

GOOSEGRASS: The herb acts as a tonic and cleanser, and helps to prevent dandruff.

HENNA: Conditioner and red hair-colourant.

HORSETAIL: Stems and branches strengthen hair.

LIME: The flowers soften and cleanse.

MARIGOLD: The petals lighten the hair colour.

NASTURTIUM: The leaves help hair growth.

PARSLEY: The leaves and stems enrich hair colour and give lustre.

ROSEMARY: The best all-round hair tonic and conditioner. The leaves and flowering tops give lustre and body, and slightly darken the hair.

SAGE: The leaves act as a tonic and conditioner, and also darken the hair.

SOUTHERNWOOD: The leaves encourage hair growth and help to prevent dandruff.

STINGING NETTLE: The leaves help to prevent dandruff and improve the condition and growth of the hair.

WITCH HAZEL: The leaves and bark are astringent and cleansing.

egg & lemon shampoo bar

The following recipe is a personal favourite that deals well with my fine, flyaway hair. I use this without a conditioner because the olive oil leaves my hair silky-soft.

shampoo style
- ❏ quick to lather
- ❏ soft on the scalp
- ❏ leaves hair glossy

28oz (792g) olive oil
2 egg yolks
2oz (57g) beeswax
2oz (57g) creamed coconut
9½oz (269g) distilled or spring water

4oz (113g) sodium hydroxide (caustic soda/lye)
2 tbsp (30g) lemon essential oil
1 tsp (5g) vitamin E oil

Grease the inside of your individual or slab mould. Set aside 1oz (28g) of olive oil and whisk this up with the egg yolks. Place the remaining olive oil, beeswax and creamed coconut in a stainless steel or enamel pot over a low heat. Pour the water into a heavy glass or plastic bowl or jug. Wearing rubber gloves and eye protection, add the sodium hydroxide to the water and stir until dissolved. When the oils have melted, remove them from the heat.

Place one sugar thermometer in the oils and one in the caustic solution. When both thermometers reach an equal temperature between 120°F (49°C) and 140°F (60°C), pour the caustic solution into the oil. (See pages 31-2). Stir until the mixture reaches trace – about 35 minutes.

Whisk in the egg/olive oil mixture a little at a time, then stir in the essential oil and vitamin E. Pour immediately into the moulds and cover. Leave to set for 24 hours or until the shampoo becomes solid. Wearing rubber gloves, remove the shampoo bar from the mould and cut into slices. Cover and leave to cure for four weeks before use.

parsley & lemon hair rinse

Parsley acts as a brightener for dull hair and is a useful herb to incorporate in your final rinse. Add some stinging nettles and you will also protect your hair from dandruff.

2 tbsp (30g) fresh, chopped stinging nettles
2 tbsp (30g) fresh, chopped parsley
juice from half a lemon
1 pint (½ litre) distilled, spring or rain water

Place the herbs in a muslin bag. Add the lemon juice to the water and place in a saucepan, add the bag of herbs and bring to the boil. Simmer for 15 minutes, then leave to cool for a further 40 minutes. Remove the herbs and use the solution as a final rinse after shampooing.

from top clockwise: natural wonder bar (recipe on page 47) also a great shampoo bar, parsley & lemon hair rinse, egg & lemon shampoo bar

special effects

Once you have mastered the basics of soapmaking you will no doubt be ready to experiment with appearance-enhancing techniques. Here are some ideas to start you off.

DECORATIVE MOULDS: There are many small decorative moulds on the market designed for making both guest soaps and candy. These can be glued to the surface of a plain, oblong, full-sized bar of soap to create a third dimension. Wait until both large and small bars have hardened and then glue one to the other with some newly traced or rebatched soap.

ICING: Traced soap has a similar consistency to glacé icing and can be pushed successfully through a piping bag to create squiggles and flowers. The texture of the soap has to be just right and I have had the greatest success using small quantities of rebatched soap for this purpose. If the soap is a little thick, add a few drops of glycerine to the mixture. Shapes can be cut from a slice of fresh soap with a sharp knife and then glued to the surface of a hard bar of soap using a small amount of melted soap mixture. You can create leaves, fishes, hearts or any shape that takes your fancy. You can also add stripes, spots and bows using the same method.

layered soaps

IMPRINTS: Imprints can be made in the surface of your soap using a rubber stamp, a woodcut or a leatherworking or sealing wax stamp. Impress the soap with the stamp before it has fully hardened.

LAYERING: One of the simplest and most effective techniques is the layering of different coloured soaps in a single bar. This technique has been described earlier in both the Creamy Coconut Soaps and the Honey and Beeswax Soaps but the variations on this theme are endless. When making a batch of soap there is inevitably a small quantity left over from a full mould and this can be used to make a layer for a special bar of soap. Select a small square or oblong container, and each time you make a coloured, transparent or textured batch, add another layer of leftovers to the mould. You can also create a scrubby bottom layer to your soap by pouring it over a base of oatmeal or tapioca. Another fun idea is to cut a square of loofah and place it in the bottom of your mould. Pour your soap on top and you have a loofah and soap bar in one.

marbled soaps

MARBLING: This effect is created by mixing two different colours of soap in the mould at once. This can be done by making a white soap and dividing it at trace before adding separate colourings. You could also rebatch two different colours of soap or make a new batch for the base soap and rebatch some coloured leftovers for the contrast. Whichever approach you take, your base soap should be poured into the mould first. The second step is to trickle lines of contrasting soap over the surface of the filled mould and then carefully fold it into the main batch with a fork. Run the fork over the surface of the mixture to create interesting marbled patterns. Do not stir vigorously or the two colours will mix.

PRESSED FLOWERS: These are a pretty addition to the surface of any bar of soap. Wet the soap and press the flowerheads into position. Then melt a little white candle wax in a double-boiler and brush it over the surface of the flowerheads. In time, the flowerheads will obviously wash off but the candle wax will keep them in place for quite a while.

STENCILLING: Paper and plastic stencils can be used to paint a design on the top of your soap. Secure the stencil to the top of a cured bar of plain soap and paint over this with a contrasting colour of soap.

TUTTI FRUTTI: Small chunks of leftover coloured soap can be added to a plain batch to create extremely pretty bars of soap. Make a batch of uncoloured soap and, when it has completely traced, scatter in two cupfuls of coloured soap cut into shapes, chunks or strips. Stir the soap well and pour into the mould. If the basic soap mix is too thin the chunks will sink to the bottom so you need a good trace before adding them. For a special effect, use coloured, transparent soap pieces in a plain white soap.

packaging soaps

Soapmaking gives you the opportunity to show how creative you can be. Once you have produced your soap, cut it into the shapes you require and decorated it, you are now ready to experiment with different styles of packaging. During the curing stages, soap has a tendency to sweat and will also shrink as the moisture evaporates. For this reason, leave your soap as long as you possibly can before you add any fancy wrappings. Keep an eye open for interesting scraps of materials, fancy trims and ribbons. The possibilities are endless and I am sure you will soon discover many new and creative ideas for packaging your soaps.

BASKETS AND BOXES: Gifts are often presented in small boxes and baskets, and these can be recycled to hold either a single bar of soap or a small collection of them. Keep packaging materials such as shredded papers and wood wool to serve as a 'nest' for your soap.

CLINGFILM: Many soapmakers choose to cover their soaps in clingfilm or shrink-wrap. To those who love the natural look this practice is rather unappealing but there are some very good reasons for doing it. Soaps that are not completely cured will attract dust and clingfilm will obviously protect them from this. It also helps to retain the scent. If you are intending to supply your soap to a shop, unless it is a really earthy establishment, film-wrapped soaps will remain looking good on the shelf for considerably longer than unwrapped ones. The film can be drawn around the soap to meet in the centre of the bar and secured with a sticky label which could be printed with your logo and/or a list of the ingredients. If you have a computer, there are many labelling programs available with ready-made graphics that you can adapt to create your own image.

CORRUGATED CARDBOARD: This is a very useful packaging material that will highlight the natural look of your soap. Cut a strip to the same depth and diameter as your circular bar of soap and wrap it around the outer edge. Secure with raffia. This will give your soap an interesting 'cartwheel' effect. This technique also works well when wrapping a large semicircle of soap.

FABRIC AND PAPER: Little soap parcels can be made by wrapping the soap in fabric or interesting paper. You can also cut ball-bands from fabric and paper so that the main body of your soap is visible. Secure the ball-band with a small piece of adhesive tape or a sticky label.

LEAVES: Soaps that will not remain wrapped for too long look wonderful parcelled in leaves, particularly the outer leaves of a cob of corn. These can be secured with raffia or alternatively with a length of pliable stem from a plant such as honeysuckle.

mystic soap (recipe on page 66)

MUSLIN AND CALICO: These have a nice, natural feel and the softness of muslin gives your soap a delicate look. Cut the edges with pinking sheers and draw a square of muslin up to the centre point of a circular bar of soap. Secure with raffia or ribbon. Create a drawstring bag by hemming the top and bottom of an oblong of calico, stitching up the sides and threading string through the hems so that the bag gathers. You might also like to rubber-stamp the front of the bag with the initials of the recipient of your soap or with festive or birthday greetings stamps.

RAFFIA: If your soap is intended as a gift for a friend you can be much more adventurous with your packaging. One of the most useful cheap packaging materials you can buy is a skein of natural raffia. This can be used to secure paper or fabric wrappings, knot and hang several bars together or it can be used by itself, wrapped numerous times around a bar of soap to create a ball-band effect. Dyed raffia looks very pretty but the colour tends to bleed on to the soap so make sure it is properly cured first.

SCALLOP SHELLS: These are free from many fishmongers (especially if you are buying something at the same time) and make interesting soap dishes for guest soaps. Add a sprinkling of real shells and/or pebbles and hold the arrangement in place with clingfilm.

troubleshooting guide

As I have said before, soapmaking is not a precise art, and while all the recipes in this book have been tried and tested, you may experience some unexpected reactions. Nine times out of ten, failed batches are due to inaccurate measuring of the ingredients. This is easily done, so when preparing batches do give the matter your full attention. Here is a list of common problems and how you should deal with them.

CRUMBLY SOAP: This can be caused by too little water. Your final soap will be difficult to cut without breaking and could prove to be quite harsh. Your options here are to rebatch the soap (see page 18) or to grate it and use it as laundry soap.

CURDLING: If you have ever poured sour milk into your tea you will have a good idea of the visual appearance of curdling. This is quite common in soaps containing milk and these can successfully be whisked into a smooth mixture. Use an electric whisk to do this and work fast. Be prepared to pour the soap quite quickly as trace will speed up considerably. Curdling sometimes occurs when you mix the fats and sodium hydroxide (caustic soda/lye) at a very high temperature.

MOTTLED SOAP: I find this commonly occurs when the soap contains a high percentage of dripping (tallow). Some people like the effect and some don't – either way it's purely cosmetic and the soap is perfectly safe to use.

NO TRACE: Your soap can take hours and hours to reach trace so, if you are sure your ingredients were weighed correctly, don't worry about it. Leave it as long as you can, stirring frequently, and then pour it into the mould. It will trace eventually.

POWDERING: White powder, called soda ash, frequently forms on the surface of the soap and this is quite harmless. Scrape or wash off the powder on the soap before wrapping it. The problem can be reduced by placing clingfilm or waxed paper directly on the surface of the soap after it has been poured into the mould.

SEIZING: If your soap mixture appears to be setting in the pan it is often due to a reaction caused by fragrance or essential oils containing alcohol. Pour the soap (or spoon it) immediately into your mould and do your best to flatten the surface. Your basic soap should be fine to use, just not as pretty as it should be.

SEPARATION: This becomes apparent after you have poured your soap into the mould. A significant layer of oil or grease sits on top of the mixture. If the layer of oil is only thin, it is probably caused by the essential oils and will be reabsorbed during the curing process. If the layer is thick, you have a caustic soap that should be discarded. This has probably been caused by an excess of sodium hydroxide in the initial mixture.

SMALL BUBBLES: These are bubbles of liquid trapped in hard soap. This is caused either by excessive amounts of sodium hydroxide or inadequate stirring. The liquid in the bubbles is caustic so you should discard the soap.

SMALL WHITE CHUNKS IN SOAP: These are caused by an excess of sodium hydroxide or inadequate stirring. The white areas are caustic and the soap should be discarded.

SOFT SOAP: If the soap is still soft after several days, this could be caused by an excess of water that prolongs the time it takes the soap to harden or you may not have used enough sodium hydroxide. Leave the soap in the mould – if it hardens eventually it should be fine to use.

STUCK SOAP: If the soap will not come out of the mould, put it in the freezer for an hour or so and try again.

us stockists

Bear American Marketing
Terry L Shay – Owner
PO BOX 829
BEAR DE 19701-0829
(302) 836-4187
e-mail address:
tlshay@magpage.com
Products: many soapmaking-related
items. Bottles, jars, gift basket fill
items, factory-fresh, high-quality
cocoa butter, beeswax. Will sell to
businesses and hobbyists. E-mail
product list available. Send e-mail
request for it. Always expanding to
sell more products. Also serves
Canadian customers.

cosmetic pigments, oxides and
colour information
'The Pigment Lady'
Lori Schenkelberg
PO Box 194
Old Saybrook CT 06475

essential oils, palm and coconut,
jojoba, avocado oils
Rainbow Meadow
6943 Clarklake Road
Jackson, MI 49201
517-764-4170
e-mail: rainbow@sojourn.com

fragrance oils
Sweet Cakes Soapmaking Supplies
Linda Jines, Proprietor
39 Brookdale Road
Bloomfield, NJ 07003
(201) 338-9830

lye, fats, soap fragrance,
soap colour
Sun Feather Soapmaking Supply
HCR 84 Box 60-A
Potsdam NY 13676
800 771-7627

moulds
Martin Creative Moulds
PO Box 101, Black Creek
BC V9J 1K8
www.martincreative.com

uk stockists

base oils – coconut, palm,
vegetable, etc.
William Hodgson & Co.
Churchgate House
56 Oxford Street
Manchester M1 6EU
0161 236 3631
Minimum 12.5-kilo blocks

cosmetic pigments and oxides
The Soapmakers Store
Unit 13, Lawson Hunt Estate
Guildford Road
Broadbridge Heath
Horsham
West Sussex, RH12 1LD
0870 240 1251
www.soapmakers-store.com

essential and fragrance oils
Amphora Aromatics Ltd
36 Cotham Hill
Cotham
Bristol BS6 6LA
0117 908 7770
http://dialspace.dial.pipex.com/
amphora_aromatics/

Sheabutter Cottage
Unit 3, Sonning Farm
Charvillane
Reading
Berkshire, RG4 6TH
0118 969 3830
www.akuawood.co.uk

Essentially Oils
8 Mount Farm
Junction Road
Churchill, Chipping Norton
Oxfordshire OX7 6NP
01608 659544
sales@essentiallyoils.com

fancy soap models, clear soap
base and colourants
House of Crafts
62 Knighton Lane
Leicester LE2 8BG
0116 283 8996

herbs, dried flowers, cosmetic
ingredients
Neals Yard Remedies
2 Neals Yard
Covent Garden
London WC2H 9DP
020 7379 7222

wax dye chips, rubber moulds,
glycerine compound and raffia
Fred Aldous Ltd
PO Box 135
37 Lever Street
Manchester M60 1UX
0161 236 2477

further reading

The Art of Soapmaking
Merilyn Mohr, Firefly Books
ISBN 092065603X

The Complete Soapmaker
Norma Coney, Sterling (Cassell)
ISBN 080694868X

The Fragrant Pharmacy
Valerie Ann Worwood, Bantam
ISBN 0553403974

Soap Recipes
Elaine C White, Valley Hills Press
ISBN 0963753959

The Soapmaker's Companion
Susan Miller Cavitch, Storey Publishing
ISBN 0882669656

Transparent Soapmaking
Catherine Failor, Rose City Press
ISBN 0965639002

internet resources

www.rainbowmeadow.com
Melody Upham of Rainbow Meadow
hosts the soapmakers' list and also
supplies many soapmaking
ingredients that can be bought by
credit card. To join her soaplist send
an e-mail to
Majordomo@UserHome.com
in the body of the text type only
subscribe soap.

lott@nfx.net
e-mail Teresa Lott and request a
copy of her free but most excellent
lye calculator that will work with
various spreadsheet programs.

www.sweetcakes.com
This address will take you to Linda
Jines's site where her wonderful
fragrance oils are listed and can be
bought by credit card.

www.motherearthherbs.com
Kathy Sedler of Mother Earth Herbs
offers an excellent selection of herbs
and soapmaker's accessories
including a wooden soap mould.
Her newsletter is also extremely
informative.

www.pigmntlady.com
'The Pigment Lady' offers useful
information and price list for
cosmetic colourants.

soapmaking courses and
holidays
www.makesoap.biz
0844 837 7317 (from the UK)
00 33 (0)553 22 66 14
(from rest of world)

www.locationdordogne.net
00 33 (0)553 22 66 14

index